THE BUSINESS CASE For DIVERSITY

FIFTH EDITION

Editorial and Production Credits

Luke Visconti Partner and Cofounder
Barbara Frankel Senior Vice President, Executive Editor
Oriol R. Gutierrez Jr. Managing Editor
Sonja Sherwood Associate Managing Editor
Robyn Heller Copy Editor

Charles Dixon III Art Director
Catherine Diaz Associate Art Director
Jermaine Jackson Graphic Designer

Written by **Gwen Moran**

Allegiant Media
570 Broad Street
Newark, NJ 07102

ISBN 0-9721112-5-5

DiversityInc

Luke Visconti Partner and Cofounder
Foulis Peacock Partner and Cofounder
Barbara Frankel Senior Vice President, Executive Editor

Editorial and Production
Luke Visconti Partner and Cofounder
Barbara Frankel Senior Vice President, Executive Editor

Oriol R. Gutierrez Jr. Managing Editor
Sonja Sherwood Associate Managing Editor

Yoji Cole Los Angeles Bureau Chief
C. Stone Brown Washington, D.C., Bureau Chief
Peter Ortiz Senior Journalist
T.J. DeGroat Senior Journalist
Brenda Velez Journalist
Carmen Cusido Journalist
Robyn Heller Copy Editor
Joe Walsh Web Production Editor

Charles Dixon III Art Director
Catherine Diaz Associate Art Director
Jermaine Jackson Graphic Designer

Shireen Khan Editorial Intern
Jennifer Millman Editorial Intern

Kathy Garris Executive Assistant to Luke Visconti
Laura Hall Executive Assistant, Editorial Department

Finance and Operations
Stuart Arnold Chief Operating Officer
Margaret Ber Accountant
Paul Bernard Business Manager
Rashonda McLemore Accounts Payable
Chetan D. Patel Accounts Receivable

Noel Arzadon IT Specialist
Katy Beekman Receptionist

Marketing and Web Services
Kathleen Davis Vice President, Marketing
Jennifer Dixon Atherley Director, Web Services
Krish Mandal Senior Manager, Web Services
Ingrid Arnold Marketing/Circulation Assistant
Rachelle Pachtman Public Relations

DiversityInc Careers
Carolynn L. Johnson Director, DiversityInc Career Center
Cassandra Crawford Account Executive, Career Center
Cliff Fyle Account Executive, Career Center

DiversityInc Benchmarking
Luis Munoz Vice President, General Manager
Shane Nelson Manager, Benchmarking Services

Sales
Foulis Peacock Partner and Cofounder

Debby Scheinholtz Account Director
Gail Zoppo Director of Advertorial Sections
Marc Mordoh Account Executive

Kimberly Stewart Manager, Customer Service
Kimiko Baugh Customer Service Representative

Cecilia Fernandez Executive Assistant to Foulis Peacock
Eamon O'Donnell Sales Assistant

Editorial & Business Office
DiversityInc
570 Broad Street
Newark, NJ 07102

Editorial: Editor@DiversityInc.com
Sales: Advertising@DiversityInc.com

Table of Contents

The United States is undergoing a profound and deep-rooted metamorphosis in its population, its culture and the very manner in which business is conducted. This transformation very well may be the greatest cultural and economic shift this country ever has known.

Diversity, defined as an inclusive work force, marketplace and business community (suppliers, partners and investors), is the nexus of this change.

To successfully compete in the United States and globally, companies must have effective and aggressive diversity management. The evidence to corroborate this statement can be found in the balance sheets of the Top 50 Companies for Diversity. The repercussions of ignoring diversity are apparent in the closed factories and empty offices of their competitors.

Put simply, diversity is all about human relations. As this country's populace undergoes dramatic demographic changes, companies must reflect the changing population within the ranks of their employees and managers to reach their customers. Increasingly, the faces of our

Introduction

work force, our suppliers and our investors are faces of color, faces of women, faces of individuals with disabilities, faces of gay, lesbian, bisexual and transgender individuals, faces of older workers. By integrating these people into the workplace, companies vigorously tailor their outreach and offerings to fit the needs of shifting cultural priorities.

At DiversityInc, we prove the bottom-line benefits of integrating diversity into every facet of business, especially the line functions directly related to revenue.

The DiversityInc Top 50 Companies for Diversity list is the most visible way to demonstrate, once and for all, how critical effective diversity management is to business success. By ranking the diversity initiatives of America's top companies each year, using strictly empirical data, we show how these businesses are benefiting from the myriad opportunities a diverse work force brings to them, from capturing new sales opportunities to retaining more of the best employees and to effectively competing globally on a planet that is 80 percent non-white.

THE DIVERSITYINC TOP 50 COMPANIES FOR DIVERSITY

The 2005 DiversityInc Top 50 Companies for Diversity list marked the fifth year of this increasingly competitive ranking, with 203 companies—up 72 percent from two years ago—completing an exhaustive survey of 230 questions. The survey was organized in four areas:

CEO Commitment
Human Capital
Corporate Communications (internal and external)
Supplier Diversity

The DiversityInc Top 50 Companies for Diversity list is the only compilation of national, substantial and valid metrics that objectively assesses diversity success. All publicly traded companies in The DiversityInc Top 50 Companies for Diversity have been placed in a stock index, which is calculated by Standard & Poor's. When examined over a 10-year period, with dividends reinvested, The DiversityInc Top 50 Companies for Diversity Index yields a 23.5 percent higher return than the Standard & Poor's 500.

In addition to The DiversityInc Top 50 Companies for Diversity, participating companies also competed for the survey's specialty lists:

The Top 10 Companies for Recruitment & Retention
The Top 10 Companies for Supplier Diversity
The Top 10 Companies for African Americans
The Top 10 Companies for Latinos
The Top 10 Companies for Asian Americans
The Top 10 Companies for Women Executives
The Top 10 Companies for GLBT Employees
The Top 10 Companies for People With Disabilities
25 Noteworthy Companies

WHY DO WE NEED THIS BOOK?

Unfortunately, there still are many companies that view diversity initiatives as philanthropic efforts or, worse, ignore them entirely. This book, as its title indicates, demonstrates the concrete business reasons for cultivating and maintaining a diverse work force, supply chain, customer base and investor community.

Still, convincing leaders of U.S. businesses requires evidence. Here, we lay out why diversity initiatives are necessary. In addition to presenting demographic information, we show how diversity leads to positive change and innovation. Readers will find real-world examples from companies from the DiversityInc Top 50 list, as well as the costs and return on investment that can be expected. Managers who need the cold, hard facts to support a proposal for increased diversity will find them here.

HOW TO USE THIS BOOK

The Fifth Edition of *The Business Case for Diversity* is entirely updated and revised. Our narrative approach lays out specific facts and figures to support the importance of workplace diversity. Clear chapter titles will direct you to the specific information you need.

The fifth edition also includes tools that will be helpful to launching and measuring your own initiatives. A series of checklists and case studies help you evaluate your own diversity initiatives and learn specific solutions from America's top companies, sharing how they implemented various elements of their diversity initiatives.

The goal of this book is to provide hard, irrefutable proof of the business benefits of diversity. We prove that diversity is a sign of a well-managed company that is poised to take advantage of opportunities and realize its fullest potential.

Luke Visconti
Foulis Peacock
Partners and Cofounders
DiversityInc

Mention diversity and most corporate leaders will nod their heads and agree that it's a good thing. Still, too often, business diversity initiatives have been categorized in the same manner as corporate giving and office philanthropy—a nice thing to do with some secondary bottom-line benefits but not essential to the well-being of the business.

That's entirely wrong. Diversity is essential for companies to survive and thrive in today's competitive business environment. The introduction of different voices, with different perspectives, backgrounds, priorities and orientations, helps companies identify opportunities and succeed in new markets. As U.S. demographics change and global economic forces have a greater impact on every area of business, it's essential that companies respond with a work force that can reach a changing customer base and with people who understand the changes that are taking place. This book makes the business case for diversity, but first, we need to cover some of the basics.

CHAPTER 1

Why Diversity?

WHAT IS DIVERSITY?

Diversity has many definitions. At its core, it means embracing differences. For the purposes of this book and addressing diversity in the workplace, diversity is defined in terms of people—measurable human capital, specifically, groups of people who have not traditionally been part of the workplace majority. These groups include: blacks; Latinos; Asian Americans; Native Americans; women in executive roles; individuals with disabilities; and gay, lesbian, bisexual and transgender (GLBT) people.

OUR CHANGING DEMOGRAPHICS

People of color are expected to make up 52.3 percent of the U.S. population by 2050.[1] This represents a significant shift in the country's cultural, racial and ethnic mix.

A few states, most recently Texas, already have reached "majority minority" status, where the number of single-race, non-Hispanic whites is lower than the population of other races and ethnicities combined. These include California, District of Columbia, Hawaii and New Mexico, with Texas edging closer with a 49.5 percent population of people of color.[2] For companies located within or marketing to these states, understanding these demographic changes is critical to increasing, or even maintaining, market share and attracting the best-qualified employees.

U.S. Population Totals by Race/Ethnicity
(In millions)

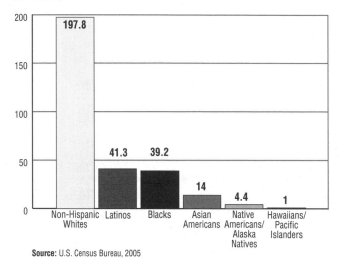

Source: U.S. Census Bureau, 2005

This dramatic shift means that the United States has a different societal makeup, and while people of color often are called minorities, that now is a misnomer in many places.

In addition, more women than ever are in the work force and in increasingly important roles, individuals with disabilities are being recognized for their contributions to companies nationwide, and gay, lesbian, bisexual and transgender individuals are experiencing greater acceptance, especially as corporations lead the way in offering these employees domestic-partner benefits.

Companies that have cultivated a diverse base of employees will be poised to understand the cultural nuances of various population sectors, enabling them to recognize new opportunities in the marketplace. We already are seeing savvy business leaders studying the needs and desires of these sectors and creating products and services for niche cultural markets, such as Volvo marketing its products to gay and lesbian families and Frito-Lay developing snack foods with traditional Latin flavors and directing marketing campaigns toward blacks. To understand the growth of these population sectors, it's important to take a closer look at the facts and factors driving their growth.

...diversity is defined in terms of people–measurable human capital, specifically, groups of people who have not traditionally been part of the workplace majority.

6

BLACKS

More than 13 percent of the U.S. population—a total of 39.2 million people—is black.[3] While this sector's gains in spending power aren't as big as Latinos', blacks will double their buying power between 1990 and 2009. This increase is powered not only by population growth but by a greater availability of jobs and the increasing rate at which blacks are launching or expanding their own businesses. Compared with whites, a larger proportion of blacks are entering the work force for the first time or climbing the company ladder, further boosting their household income.[4]

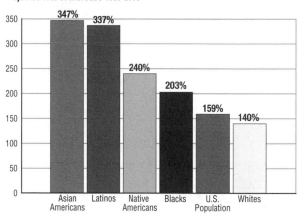

Buying Power by Race
Projected rate of increase 1990-2009

Source: University of Georgia's Selig Center for Economic Growth

More than 37 percent of the buying power among blacks is centered in the states with the top five black markets: New York, California, Texas, Georgia and Florida.[5]

While the average of the 14 million black households in the United States[6] spent 70 percent of what the overall average U.S. household spent, there were a number of key areas in which blacks spent more, including telephone services, utilities, property rentals, clothing for young children, and footwear.[7] This tells us that examining the increases in buying power by region and by category of expenditures can lead companies to identify opportunities to service the unique needs of these markets.

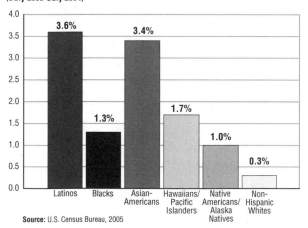

Percentage Growth by Race/Ethnicity
(July 2003-July 2004)

Source: U.S. Census Bureau, 2005

LATINOS

Latinos, already the largest segment of people of color and the fastest-growing population segment, will more than triple their discretionary income between 1990 and 2009. Their buying power is projected to eclipse that of blacks, who will double their discretionary income over the same period of time.

The population growth of Latinos, to a total of 41.3 million, accounted for half of the nation's population growth in the period between July 2003 and July 2004.[8] This growth is driven by a combination of higher birth rates, as well as strong immigration numbers, with the greatest numbers of Latin immigrants coming from Mexico, Cuba and El Salvador.[9] Latinos also are benefiting from better job opportunities. Young Latinos are entering the work force at increasingly higher percentages and are earning increases in job responsibility and pay, which is bumping up their buying power.[10]

Because this segment is relatively young, translating to entry-level employees who will join the work force and work their way up the ranks of their companies, the segment will continue to increase its buying power as these workers become more affluent.

To understand the Latino market, it's critical to understand the difference between acculturated, bicultural and unacculturated Latinos. These segments also apply to many other immigrant populations in the United States.[11]

Messages that will appeal to an unacculturated individual are likely to be very different than those that will appeal to an acculturated audience.

Unacculturated: This group consists of foreign-born Latinos who recently have arrived in the United States, usually as adults. Their primary language is Spanish, and their affinity for products and services is still deeply rooted in their experiences in their Latin American homelands.[12]

Bicultural: Bicultural Latinos have fully adapted to U.S. culture; however, they still are connected to their Latino heritage. They are comfortable speaking both English and Spanish and have grown up exposed to both cultures. Most arrived in the United States at an early age; however, they continue to identify themselves by their parents' nationality.[13]

Acculturated: Consisting mainly of Latinos who are second-generation or greater, they are most comfortable speaking English at work or in social settings. Their values and perceptions are most like the general U.S. consumer market.[14] Within the acculturated Latino segment, there is a trend toward retro-acculturation—the rediscovery of one's heritage—which has embraced cultural influences in food, music and other elements of their Latino heritage.[15]

...examining the increases in buying power by region and by category of expenditures can lead companies to identify opportunities to service the unique needs of these markets.

It's important to understand the differences among these immigrant populations in order to communicate to them effectively. Messages that will appeal to an unacculturated individual are likely to be very different than those that will appeal to an acculturated audience.

ASIAN AMERICANS

There are nearly 14 million people of Asian heritage living in the United States. Asian Americans (a term used by DiversityInc to describe both immigrant and U.S.-born Asians) represent East Asian nations such as China, Japan and Korea; South Asian countries such as India, Pakistan and Nepal; and Southeast Asian nations such as Thailand, Vietnam and Malaysia.[16] The Census Bureau estimates that 13.5 million U.S. residents are Asian American or Asian in combination with one or more other races, comprising 5 percent of the total population, and representing a 12.5 percent surge between 2000 and 2004.[17] California has both the largest population (4.6 million) and the largest numerical increase (367,100) of people of this group since April 2000; Hawaii is the state where Asians make up the highest proportion of the total population (58 percent).[18]

Asian Americans will double in population and spending

Asian-American Buying Power

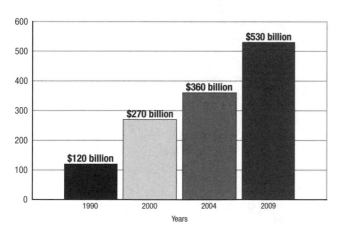

Source: College Board, U.S. Census Bureau, University of Georgia's Selig Center For Economic Growth

power between 1990 and 2009. Like other market segments, Asian Americans will benefit from the strong economy. However, Asian Americans also are benefiting from more education, which leads to employment in management or higher-level positions.[19] Fifty percent of Asian Americans age 25 and older have a bachelor's degree or higher level of education, compared to 27 percent of the total population.

Asian Americans have the highest proportion of college graduates of any race or ethnic group in the country. Eighty-eight percent of Asian Americans ages 25 and older are high-school graduates versus 85 percent of the general population in this age group, and 19 percent have an advanced degree (e.g., master's, Ph.D., M.D. or J.D.). The corresponding rate for all adults in the age group is 9 percent.[20] Continued strong immigration among this diverse segment, which includes many subgroups, also is impacting buying power.[21]

This group's spending power is very geographically focused when compared with the overall consumer market. In 2004, the 10 states with the largest Asian-American consumer markets made up 62.1 percent and 77 percent of the Asian buying power, respectively.[22] Again, examining regional growth of multicultural markets can help companies determine where specific opportunities lie.

NATIVE AMERICANS

Another segment of the U.S. population that will increase in spending power is the Native American market, which is projected to grow by an astounding 53.1 percent in the period between 1990 and 2009— more than four times that of the general population.[23] Despite this fast-paced growth, the Native American population only will increase from 0.8 percent of the total population in 1990 to 1 percent in 2009.[24] This is the only ethnic/racial market whose growth is not propelled by immigration but solely by birth rate.

Native Americans are another group benefiting from more jobs and increased levels of entrepreneurship, as well as fast population-growth trends.[25] Between 1997 and 2004, businesses owned by Native American women and Asian Americans each grew 69 percent.[26] Still, Native Americans only are expected to make up 0.6 percent of U.S. buying power in 2009, up slightly from their 0.5 percent share in 1990.[27]

GAY, LESBIAN, BISEXUAL AND TRANSGENDER PEOPLE

The gay, lesbian, bisexual and transgender (GLBT) market remains a relatively untapped market. A 2004 report by market-research publisher Packaged Facts estimated the buying power of this group at $610 billion in 2005.[28]

In addition, GLBTs are among the most loyal consumers, deliberately choosing companies with inclusive policies and outreach. A December 2004 survey by Harris Interactive found that 70 percent of GLBT respondents said they are extremely or very likely to consider a brand that provides workplace benefits for all of their employees, including gays and lesbians, and nearly two-thirds (64 percent) of respondents said that they are likely to consider purchasing household products and services from companies that market directly to GLBT markets over competing brands that do not.

Volvo was savvy enough to go after the GLBT market full-force in an ad campaign that was launched in 2003 and ran through 2004. Introducing its new sport utility vehicle to the GLBT audience, the award-winning "Starting a Family" print ad also featured the company's C70 convertible. The headline read, "Whether You're Starting a Family or Creating One as You Go."

In developing the campaign, Volvo had to address the difficulty of measuring the GLBT audience. Members of this segment may not self-identify. Prior to Census 2000, activists urged gays and lesbians to check "unmarried partner" rather than "roommates" or "other non-relative."

The GLBT Community in the United States

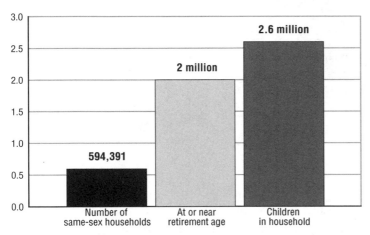

Source: Report, "The U.S. Gay and Lesbian Community," 2004; and U.S. Census Bureau, "Married-Couple and Unmarried-Partner Households 2000," February 2003.

Volvo used online survey methods to gather information about GLBT automotive consumers, resulting in 1,000 GLBT consumers and an additional 1,000 heterosexual consumers participating in online polling of their vehicle-purchasing preferences. Volvo used the results to define the areas of concentration needed to appeal to GLBT consumers.

Employment Rates of People With Disabilities

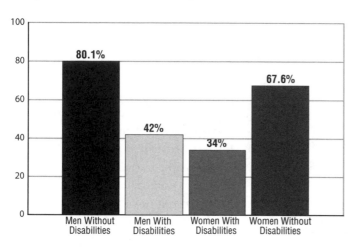

Source: U.S. Census Bureau

PEOPLE WITH DISABILITIES

While stereotypes portray the market for people with disabilities as being heavily unemployed and underwhelming as an economic force, individuals with disabilities comprise a market that is 54-million-people strong, maintains an aggregate income that now exceeds $1 trillion and boasts $220 billion in discretionary spending power.[29]

Another reason that this group is such an attractive segment is that marketing to people with disabilities means reaching caregivers and families as well. Marketing programs aimed at people with disabilities can reach as many as four out of every 10 consumers.[30]

AGING AMERICANS

On July 1, 2004, the number of people age 65 and older in the United States hit 36.3 million, or 12 percent of the total population. As baby boomers—those individuals born between 1946 and 1964—become older, it's time to look at the impact that aging Americans have in the marketplace and to give them the attention they deserve.

The baby-boomer population is the most diverse group when compared with previous generations. Thirty percent of the segment is comprised of people of color.

They also have a viable pool of workers, which is good news for companies concerned about the potential of a labor shortage. A survey conducted by AARP shows that nearly 40 percent of workers age 50 and older expressed an interest in working part time instead of retiring, and current retirees said they would have been interested in a phased retirement had it been available to them. Both groups agreed that more flexible options, such as part-time work and phased retirement, would have kept them in the work force longer.[31] Of the 65+ population, 12.5 percent, or 4.5 million, still are employed or actively seeking employment.[32]

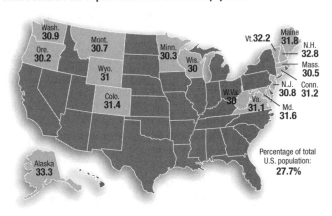

Boomer States
Where boomers are 30 percent or more of the state population

Wash. **30.9**
Ore. **30.2**
Mont. **30.7**
Minn. **30.3**
Wis. **30**
Vt. **32.2**
Maine **31.8**
N.H. **32.8**
Mass. **30.5**
Conn. **31.2**
N.J. **30.8**
Wyo. **31**
Colo. **31.4**
W.Va **30**
Va. **31.1**
Md. **31.6**
Alaska **33.3**

Percentage of total U.S. population: **27.7%**

Source: MetLife Mature Market Institute, U.S. Census Bureau

WOMEN

While women are not an "emerging" market, they are a powerful one, responsible for as much as 83 percent of all consumer purchases.

Women generate about $5 trillion in spending—about half of the U.S. gross domestic product.[33]

Women of color are a buying powerhouse. According to a 2004 report by market-research firm Packaged Facts, the combined group of black, Asian-American and Latina women has grown almost 40 percent between 1995 and 2003 versus the population of white women, which grew a mere 7 percent.[34] These 32

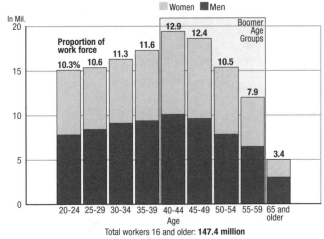

Boomers in the Work Force

Women Men

In Mil.

Proportion of work force

10.3% 10.6 11.3 11.6 12.9 12.4 Boomer Age Groups 10.5

7.9

3.4

20-24 25-29 30-34 35-39 40-44 45-49 50-54 55-59 65 and older

Age

Total workers 16 and older: **147.4 million**

Source: U.S. Census Bureau, 2000

million women hold nearly $723 billion in purchasing power, and the report estimates that total will exceed $1 trillion by 2008.[35]

DIVERSITY: THE SIGN OF A WELL-MANAGED COMPANY

Business attitudes toward diversity are changing rapidly. When DiversityInc launched its magazine in 2002, we estimated that only 5 percent of Fortune 500 companies had made a significant commitment to diversity initiatives. By this year, we estimated that as many as 15 percent of Fortune 500 companies had made diversity initiatives a priority, as demonstrated by participation in The 2005 DiversityInc Top 50 Companies for Diversity competition, up 72 percent in 2005 from two years earlier, with 203 companies participating this year.

DiversityInc always has maintained that such programs are the sign of a well-managed company. It was not surprising when The 2005 DiversityInc Top 50 Companies for Diversity Index revealed that the 43 publicly traded companies on the list held their value better than other indexes, the Standard & Poor's 500, the Dow Jones Industrial Average and the Nasdaq 100.[36] The DiversityInc Top 50 Companies for Diversity had a 23.5 percent higher return than the S&P 500 over 10 years with dividends reinvested.[37]

The positive effects of an inclusive culture essentially fall into four broad categories: management, human capital, internal and external marketing and supplier relations.

MANAGEMENT

When the highest levels of management are involved in diversity initiatives, it means that they understand the bottom-line benefits of being inclusive. When senior management is directly involved with diversity initiatives, that sends a resounding signal to all stakeholders that the corporate leadership cares about programs that enable them to reach the broadest possible markets with the best possible human assets. A strong diversity initiative is the hallmark of an organization that makes its employees and its customers feel valued.

Strong companies continually measure themselves against their competition and try to improve. That reason is cited time and time again by corporate leaders when asked why they participate in The DiversityInc

Top 50 Companies for Diversity survey. One look at the corporate leaders that are ranked on The 2005 DiversityInc Top 50 Companies for Diversity list indicates that the correlation between strong corporate management and strong diversity initiatives is no coincidence.

HUMAN CAPITAL

Companies that value diversity cultivate the best possible employee base because of the wide pool of candidates that they attract, and they retain all employees at a far higher rate, including white employees. Among the DiversityInc Top 10 Companies for Recruitment & Retention, retention rates for whites, Latinos, Asian Americans and women all were in the 90 percent range.[38]

The positive effects of an inclusive culture essentially fall into four broad categories: management, human capital, internal and external marketing and supplier relations.

Meanwhile, for companies ranked 41–50 on The DiversityInc Top 50 Companies for Diversity list, retention rates dropped to between 65 percent and 75 percent. Companies that ranked higher than 91 plummet to as low as 50 percent retention, with the highest loss in black and Latino workers. What does this tell us? Talented black and Latino employees are far more willing to jump ship, leaving companies without critical connections to those communities and stuck with a work force of potential underperformers.[39]

MARKETING AND OUTREACH

Companies such as Marriott (No. 12 on The 2005 DiversityInc Top 50 Companies for Diversity list) make it a point to communicate their commitment to diversity, to both their external and internal audiences. Their commitment to their inclusive programs is a benefit to both employees and customers. From corporate mission statements that reflect the importance of diversity within the organization to marketing campaigns that target specific and diverse market segments, companies that take their inclusive culture seriously—and tell people about it—find that they attract a loyal base of employees and customers who appreciate being acknowledged and valued.

"Customers are getting to the point where they're asking what we're doing about it. Diversity is an important piece of securing business with outside organizations; so many times, we include information on our diversity practices," says Maruiel Perkins-Chavis, Marriott's vice president, workforce effectiveness and diversity.[40]

DIVERSITY

Every successful company relies on a network of suppliers to help it operate more smoothly and to enhance its ability to deliver products and services to the marketplace. Well-managed companies seek out the best possible suppliers from a diverse pool of options.

Just as companies that cultivate diverse employee pools are poised to take advantage of marketplace opportunities, companies that cultivate diverse supplier pools are able to better serve their customers. These business partners bring unique perspectives to the company. Companies that have strong supplier-diversity initiatives benefit from making deep and lasting inroads into emerging markets.

In the following chapters, we'll examine these four areas more closely and look specifically at what it takes to achieve them. We'll show how inclusive companies are enjoying significant benefits from their diversity initiatives.

[1] 2000 U.S. Census

[2] Census Bureau estimates, released 9/30/04

[3] Census Bureau

[4] Selig Report, page 3

[5] Ibid

[6] U.S. Census Bureau

[7] Bureau of Labor Statistics, Consumer Expenditure Survey 2003, "Table 2100. Race of Reference Person: Average Annual Expenditures and Characteristics"

[8] U.S. Census Bureau estimates, released June 9, 2005

[9] U.S. Census Bureau, "Top 10 Countries of Birth of the Foreign-Born Population: 2000"

[10] Selig Report, page 6

[11] *DiversityInc* magazine, "Culture Shock: What U.S. Companies Need to Know about Latino Consumers," by Angela Johnson Meadows, August/September 2004

[12] Ibid

[13] Ibid

[14] Ibid

[15] Ibid

[16] *DiversityInc* magazine, "To Be Asian in America," by Angela Johnson Meadows, April 2005

[17] U.S. Census Bureau, Asian/Pacific American Heritage Month, May 2005

[18] Ibid

[19] Selig Report, page 5

[20] U.S. Census Bureau, "Educational Attainment in the United States: 2003," Released June 2004

[21] Ibid

[22] Ibid

[23] Selig Report, page 4

[24] Selig Report, page 11, Share of Population

[25] Ibid

[26] Center for Women's Business Research, 2004

[27] Selig Report, page 4

[28] Packaged Facts, "The U.S. Gay and Lesbian Market," September 2004

[29] Diversityinc.com, "What Marketers Should Know About People with Disabilities," by Kipp Cheng, April 2002

[30] Solutions Marketing Group: www.disability-marketing.com/facts, accessed November 2005

[31] *DiversityInc* magazine, "Retirees Want to Work – Part Time," June 2005, page 26

[32] Census Bureau, "Employed Citizens and Weekly Hours 2003"

[33] Barletta, M. *Marketing to Women: How to Understand, Reach, and Increase Your Share of the World's Largest Market Segment* (Dearborn, 2002)

more>>>

34 U.S. Census and Packaged Facts, "Growth in Population, Multi-cultural vs. Other Women 1995-2003"

35 Packaged Facts, "The U.S. Multicultural Women Market," June 2004

36 *DiversityInc*, "How Diversity Impacts Shareholder Return," June 2005, by Yoji Cole, page 68

37 Ibid

38 DiversityInc

39 DiversityInc

40 *DiversityInc*, "Why Participate? Ask Employees, Customers, Vendors and Investors," by Angela Johnson Mcadows and Yoji Cole, June 2005

Good diversity management is all about relationships. Cultivating relationships with key stakeholders—customers, employees, investors, suppliers, business partners and community leaders—requires an environment of trust. They must believe that your company is a good steward of their interests. An organization focused on building that trust must clearly communicate its commitment to the community and to the organizations with which it does business.

For a diversity initiative to create and nurture a sense of trust, a company must receive engaged support from the CEO and senior management. Without that leadership, continued support and strong involvement of the CEO, no corporate diversity initiative can succeed. CEO buy-in is essential for both empowering diversity-management leadership to create positive change and empowering employees to work to the best of their abilities to contribute to a culture of diversity.

CHAPTER 2

Starting at the Top:

The Importance of C-Level and Board Buy-In

Cultivation of trust must be sincere. Companies that actually "walk their talk" by both communicating a commitment to diversity and following through with budget, actions, programs and initiatives, such as creating diversity councils, tying management compensation to diversity initiatives and launching strong supplier-diversity programs, ultimately benefit from the myriad opportunities that an inclusive culture brings. Conversely, if employees, customers and other stakeholders get a sense that diversity is just another public-relations move designed to generate a positive image but not backed by the necessary resources and leadership, such programs can backfire.

> For a diversity initiative to create and nurture a sense of trust, a company must receive engaged support from the CEO and senior management.

WHY DOES C-LEVEL AND MANAGEMENT BUY-IN MATTER?

When senior management champions diversity programs, those programs flourish within an organization. Chief diversity officers, diversity directors and other key managers who are encouraged and empowered are able to spearhead efforts to create an inclusive culture within their organizations.

While recruitment is a critical component of those efforts, valid and aggressive diversity management extends far beyond employee relations and into operations, marketing, sales, purchasing and even financial operations, since diversity management has a direct and positive impact on the bottom line. Effective diversity initiatives allow companies to understand and target emerging and untapped markets, reaching new customers and developing new product offerings. Inclusive cultures allow companies to find the best suppliers to meet their customers' needs.

With the support and commitment of management, diversity directors gain new credibility and respect, allowing them to make the significant changes necessary to create a more inclusive culture. In the following chapters, we'll examine how successful diversity initiatives are part of every sector of an organization.

DIVERSITY ON BOARD

Corporate boards have not traditionally been a good place to look for diversity. However, after the well-publicized corporate scandals at Enron, WorldCom and others, fundamental shifts are taking place in the mix of people who occupy the seats around the boardroom conference table. Now that we are entrenched in the era of Sarbanes-Oxley, corporate boards have an incentive to seek a more diverse mix of individuals to lead their corporations.[1]

However, there is a severe underrepresentation of women and people of

Board Representation

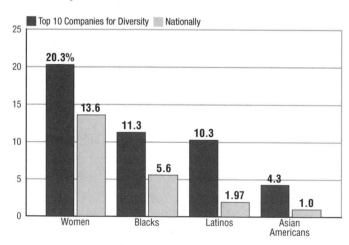

Top 10 Companies for Diversity ▪ Nationally

- Women: 20.3% / 13.6
- Blacks: 11.3 / 5.6
- Latinos: 10.3 / 1.97
- Asian Americans: 4.3 / 1.0

Source: DiversityInc, Catalyst, HARC, IRRC, Committee of 100

color on the boards of the Fortune 100, according to a recent report from Catalyst, an advisory organization focusing on the advancement of women in the workplace. As of Sept. 30, 2004, board seats on the Fortune 100 totaled 1,195. Women and individuals of color held 28.79 percent of the seats, while overall, white men held 71.21 percent of the seats.[2]

> **"What's the market, what's the geography? ... If it has its corporate headquarters somewhere in the United States but is operating world-wide and has no one on that board bringing ... a global perspective, that doesn't make sense to me."**
> –Dr. Johnnetta B. Cole, president of Bennett College for Women

Worse, the report found that among women or people of color who are part of corporate boards, many are "recycled" in that they are tapped for other board positions.[3] This means that the companies weren't actively looking for fresh voices to add to their boards but simply were turning to individuals who had been recruited for other boards.

A corporate board needs a good mix of skills and outlooks to serve its stakeholders. As stakeholders become more diverse, companies with board representation that mirrors this diversity are poised to respond to the market's needs. Quicker and more accurate responses to market shifts lead to economic rewards.[4]

The point of board diversity is to utilize the enormous breadth of knowledge held by the multitude of senior executives working throughout corporate America, its business schools and its private enterprises. Recycling the few diverse directors who already sit on boards is not utilizing the nation's population of executives of color and women to its highest potential.[5]

Yet supporters of corporate-board diversity see the increase in the number of diverse board members as promising. They add, however, that corporate boards must be as diverse as the communities in which their companies conduct business.[6]

"What's the market, what's the geography? ... If it has its corporate headquarters somewhere in the United States but is operating worldwide and has no one on that board bringing ... a global perspective, that doesn't make sense to me," says Dr. Johnnetta B. Cole, president of Bennett College for Women and the first woman of color to sit on the boards of Home Depot and Coca-Cola Enterprises. She also has sat on the board of Eastman Kodak. She currently is chair of the United Way and sits on the board of Merck & Co.[7]

Perspective is the key word. In the art world, perspective is a method employed to represent three-dimensional space on a flat surface. Perspective brings understanding of how to best present a company's products and services to an increasingly diverse population. The perspective that a director brings to the board as a person of color or as a woman usually differs from the CEO's point of view. Directors who are people of color or women are likely to have owned their own companies, so they are more attentive to labor and ethics issues than the average white-male director who spent a career in corporate America.[8]

Such personal and professional experience outside of the mainstream destroys insular thought. It naturally opens an organization to new networks, methods of recruitment, methods of attracting business partnerships and developing consumer awareness. Avoiding group-think

Is Your Company Committed to Diversity?

How can you tell if your employer is serious about inclusiveness? Effective diversity initiatives have some key elements in common. These criteria should be met:

■ Our CEO is involved in diversity programs and frequently includes messages about diversity in his or her communications.

■ The employees in our organization reflect a mix of people of different races, ethnicities, genders, ages, physical abilities and sexual orientation, at every level of the company but increasingly in the decision-maker level.

■ Recruitment programs place an emphasis on inclusive practices, such as advertising on Web sites such as DiversityInc's Career Center, college programs, and business associations targeted toward people of color, women, GLBTs and individuals with disabilities.

■ The organization makes a clear and good-faith effort to meet the needs of a diverse employee base, such as making accommodations for employees with disabilities and offering domestic-partner benefits.

■ The company examines demographic trends and consistently works toward finding ways to reach emerging markets of varying races, ethnicities, genders, ages, physical abilities and sexual orientation.

■ Diversity initiatives are tied to management-performance reviews and management compensation.

■ The organization's board of directors includes a mix of members.

■ The company has clear and

protects a company from scandal, says Michael Critelli, chairman and CEO of Pitney Bowes (No. 19 on The 2005 DiversityInc Top 50 Companies for Diversity list), whose 10-member board has four diverse directors, including a black man, a Latino and a Latina.[9]

Critelli, who chairs the National Urban League's board of trustees, understands the benefit of fresh thinking, since he, as a white man, brought racial diversity to the black organization's board.[10]

"I find that women and people of color are not coming from other boardrooms and are not CEOs, so they [bring] different perspectives," says Critelli. "Diverse executives get away from group-think and my experience in the history of different scandals … is that it is the people who challenge the prevailing way of thinking that cause scandals to be prevented or become serious."[11]

Historically, a company's board members were CEOs of other companies with which they conducted business. That tradition, however, created insular corporate boards that held the concerns of the CEO and the CEO's business partners in higher regard than the interests of the company's stakeholders. Sarbanes-Oxley, the U.S. Congres-

firm nondiscrimination policies, which include equal treatment for all employees regardless of race, ethnicity, gender, age, ability or sexual orientation.

■ The organization has an active diversity-training program.

■ The organization's succession plan includes consideration for diversity in future leadership.

■ External communications clearly state that the company values an inclusive culture and actively communicates to diverse audience segments.

■ The company solicits employee feedback about diversity initiatives and uses that information to improve its programs.

■ The company's Web site includes easy-to-find information on diversity initiatives and career opportunities for people of color, women, GLBTs and individuals with disabilities.

■ The company actively seeks diverse suppliers, including businesses owned, controlled and managed by people of color, individuals and veterans with disabilities, and women.

■ The company requires third-party certification to ensure that its suppliers meet the ownership criteria necessary to achieve supplier-diversity initiatives.

■ The company taps its multicultural knowledge base to develop new products, services, sales efforts and marketing programs for niche audiences.

■ These are some of the criteria used to evaluate companies on The DiversityInc Top 50 Companies for Diversity list. The more statements that apply to your organization, the more likely it is that diversity initiatives are well-managed and effective.

sional mandate passed in 2002 that seeks to protect investors from fraudulent accounting activities, requires companies to hire more independent directors with financial, legal and operational backgrounds, effectively forcing companies to cast wider nets.[12]

Avoiding group-think protects a company from scandal.
–Michael Critelli, chairman and CEO of Pitney Bowes

When casting their nets in fresh waters, corporate boards are more likely to catch qualified board candidates of color and women candidates. By and large, corporate America's recruiting efforts are not developed enough to seek directors who have disabilities or are gay or lesbian, but more companies are recruiting women directors and directors of color than in previous years, according to Korn/Ferry International, a Los Angeles–based executive-recruitment firm that researches the diversity of the Fortune 1000's corporate boards.[13]

Directors of color and women directors tend to think about the human side of business more than their white counterparts, says Barbara Bowles, chair of the board and CEO of The Kenwood Group, a Chicago-based investment-advisory firm she founded in 1989.

Bowles is a prime example of the talent corporate America misses when it creates barriers for people of color and women. Prior to launching The Kenwood Group, Bowles was vice president of trust investments for First National Bank of Chicago and an assistant vice president and director of investor relations at Beatrice Companies, and she served as corporate vice president at Kraft Foods (No. 10 on The 2005 DiversityInc Top 50 Companies for Diversity list).[14]

"I find that women and people of color are not coming from other boardrooms and are not CEOs, so they [bring] different perspectives." –Michael Critelli

Bowles speaks directly when sitting in the boardroom, a trait she says often is shared among board members of color and women. Another tradition among corporate boards that feature all or mostly white males is that business is conducted outside of the boardroom at golf clubs or restaurants. Often, women and people of color don't attend these events, so she makes sure her concerns are addressed at board meetings.[15] For a director's ideas to be developed, that director must have the support of other members of the board so diverse directors are not always the ones who bring up diversity issues. Other directors who may not be as personally involved with diversity as a director of color or woman director will see that the board addresses diversity issues so their issue receives support from the diverse directors. Having diverse board members informs the entire board that issues affecting people of color and women are the company's concern.[16]

"I don't need to be the one to raise diversity issues, but the fact that I'm in the room helps the issue be raised," says Bowles.[17]

Similarly, diverse corporate boards usually lead to diverse

Exceptional CEO Commitment: PepsiCo's Steve Reinemund

After a meeting with a small group of black employees in 2001, PepsiCo CEO and Chairman Steve Reinemund was shocked to receive an e-mail from an employee who said a talk he had given to her and other black employees reminded her of a plantation owner talking down to slaves.[27]

The note troubled Reinemund, but the woman's perspective also shed light on a problem he didn't know existed. Since that day, Reinemund has tried to avoid podiums. He also has helped his company cement its status as a corporate-diversity leader.[28]

CEO commitment is part of PepsiCo's success. *The Wall Street Journal* reported in April 2005 that PepsiCo credits one percentage point of its 2003 7.4 percent revenue growth (about $250 million) to new products such as guacamole-flavored Doritos and Gatorade Xtremo, designed to appeal to Latinos.[29]

In addition to tying his management team's compensation to diversity initiatives, Reinemund also assigned his team to become executive sponsors of the company's various employee groups, which offer resources for blacks, Latinos, Asian Americans, women, people with disabilities and others. The executives are expected to mentor at least three people in their group and report regularly to Reinemund and other leaders about the members' needs.[30]

senior leadership and diversity-management initiatives that seek to recruit, retain and conduct business from and with diverse communities. It is like having different friends: Once you broaden your circle of friends to include more people than just those who share your particular race or ethnic background, you become more competent in more cultures than your own. Diverse corporate boards provide a company with insight into providing competent products and services and responsible marketing to diverse communities.[18]

Moreover, directors who are women and people of color build employee morale. Through their networks, diverse directors are able to point managers in the direction of where to find top-notch talent among people of color, women, GLBTs and people with disabilities. These directors will emphasize to company management the need to

> "I don't need to be the one to raise diversity issues, but the fact that I'm in the room helps the issue be raised."–Barbara Bowles

implement developmental plans for women and employees of color, as well as mentoring plans for diverse employees. If a company wants to retain a high-performing management team, it will make sure that high-performing diverse executives see a culture at the top that supports their desire to become executives who occupy the "chief" suites. Board members of color are living testimonials to that type of support.[19]

REPORTING STRUCTURES OF CDOS, DIVERSITY DIRECTORS

The difference between a chief diversity officer (CDO) or diversity director who is effective and has an impact on the bottom line and one who is just window dressing lies in the reporting structure of the company. Companies with less successful diversity initiatives often have the

New Values: Bausch & Lomb

Riddled with layoffs, disappointing earnings and legal battles, just four years ago diversity for eye-care-product manufacturer Bausch & Lomb (B&L) was based on the old company values that only referred to race and gender. Today, the Rochester, N.Y.–based company (No. 33 on The 2005 DiversityInc Top 50 Companies for Diversity list) has made a turnaround.[21]

Its diversity initiative has progressed to cultural drivers that recruit people from different backgrounds, cultures and worldviews to bring unique perspectives and talents to the table.[22] B&L also conducts a thorough pre-assessment interview to make certain that a candidate is a good fit, as well as a follow-up interview that details the company's culture to make certain that candidates understand the culture. Once on board, an employee is required to attend an orientation session to serve as reinforcement.[23]

"We believe that that dynamic—an environment rich with ideas and expression—permits innovation, creativity and high-quality problem-solving to occur," says Clay Osborne, vice president, human resources, diversity and organizational effectiveness. They've figured out how this collective talent base can help them gain new markets.[24]

diversity director far-removed from the corner office, several reports away from the CEO, and housed in a human-resources cubicle.

To be fair, some companies understand that human-resources functions, including diversity management, are crucial to the bottom line. Those companies accord diversity directors the same respect—and demand the same kind of accountability—that line executives receive.[20]

With that kind of clout comes ability by the chief diversity officer or diversity director to have an impact that affects far more than the employee base. Such high-level positioning allows the diversity leader to spearhead other important initiatives, including supplier diversity, marketing and selling to diverse audiences, and developing programs such as affinity groups and diversity councils that harness the knowledge of a diverse employee base. By positioning the chief diversity officer or diversity director as a top-line report, a resounding message is sent throughout the company that this is a high-ranking position that deserves respect.

Companies that understand the potential of an effective diversity leader understand that this is a person who requires access across company departments and who needs the authority to make a difference in various areas of the company. The diversity director should have influence not only in recruitment and human resources but also in the development of new products and services, as well as crafting marketing and sales programs. To ensure that a company's efforts are truly reaching diverse markets and communicating inclusive messages, it is critical that the diversity director weigh in on key decisions in these areas.

PUTTING A SUCCESSFUL DIVERSITY PROGRAM IN PLACE

Among the most successful corporate diversity initiatives, all have similar components to their foundations. For the best possible outcome in creating an effective diversity program, focus on the following areas:

COMMITMENT

Before any effort is put forth into a diversity initiative, the company has to determine its level of commitment to becoming more inclusive. Senior management needs to understand the business case for creating a diversity initiative, including the benefits that an inclusive culture will bring to the company—a wider talent pool from which to recruit; firsthand knowledge and understanding of emerging markets; higher levels of retention among the best employees; working with more and varied suppliers to better deliver products and services; and the ability to recognize and target emerging markets. To achieve these benefits, the company needs to integrate diversity as part of its core business functions, determining clearly why a diversity program is necessary.

DIVERSITY LEADERSHIP

Top management and the board of directors need to pledge their support of a diversity leader who will spearhead inclusive efforts throughout the company, including recruitment and retention of a diverse employee base, identifying new opportunities in emerging markets, cultivating a diverse base of suppliers and creating a culture of inclusion where employees feel valued and accepted. When the chief diversity officer has the enthusiastic support of top management, diversity programs are far more effective.

INCLUSIVE POLICIES

Clear and well-communicated policies are essential to diversity-management success. Such policies should begin with the management stance and frequent reinforcement that diversity is a company priority and should extend to employee communication, organizational nondiscrimination policies and recruitment activities. Management-performance reviews and bonuses should be tied to clear diversity goals, which will further ensure that these policies are made a priority.

BUDGET

A company's diversity program should have a budget line attached to it, which will adequately support the resources necessary to achieve success. These items will include staff training, corporate-communications efforts and recruitment initiatives for both employees and suppliers, among others. Commitment to properly fund aggressive diversity initiatives is a hallmark of a CEO's real value of diversity.

TRAINING

Training programs for both management and staff are critically important to diversity-program success. The topic of training will be addressed more thoroughly in Chapter 4 but in most companies, management and staff need to be familiarized with all of the opportunities there are to make a company more diverse. Staff members may need training to increase their comfort level and communication skills, to make them more effective when working side by side with people who are different from them. Managers need to be trained in diversity goals and objectives, understanding that their performance will be measured, in part, by how effectively they meet those goals and objectives.

EMPLOYEE BUY-IN

Keeping your finger on the pulse of your employee base is critical to determine whether your efforts are working and to gather feedback about new opportunities for the diversity-management team. These councils are made up of employee representatives from all areas of the company and can help you mine great ideas while keeping the lines of communication open between you and your staff. Companies also should have methods to solicit employee feedback, which may include gathering information during performance reviews or anonymous suggestion.

COMMUNICATION STRATEGIES

In diversity initiatives, success fosters more success. As the word gets out that a company is serious about its inclusive policies, it will attract more diverse job applicants and suppliers. In addition, internal-communication vehicles—employee newsletters, intranet, etc.—should feature diversity-success stories and information.

Organizations can create an immediate impact by modifying the organizational mission statement to reflect a commitment to diversity. Another immediate and important action is to update Web sites to support diversity initiatives, including adding information about the organizational diversity policy, application information for candidates, and ensuring that any people who are depicted represent a diverse cross-section of employees, including people of color, women, and individuals with disabilities.[25] (See Chapter 4 for more strategies.)

MEASUREMENT MECHANISMS

From the start, make sure that tools are in place to measure and document everything that you're doing. For example, monitor representation and percentage changes, along with promotions, salaries and complaints. Monitor supplier-diversity initiatives, including percentage changes and dollar amounts. Check whether new customers in multi-cultural communities are signing on since your diversity initiatives began. Prove your case, once and for all, to senior management.[26]

[1] *DiversityInc*, "Bringing New Voices to the Board of Directors," by Yoji Cole, February 2005

[2] Catalyst, "Women and Minorities on Fortune 100 Boards," May 17, 2005

[3] Ibid

[4] *DiversityInc*, "Bringing New Voices to the Board of Directors," Yoji Cole, February 2005

[5] Ibid

[6] Ibid

[7] Ibid

[8] Ibid

[9] Ibid

[10] Ibid

[11] Ibid

[12] Ibid

[13] Ibid

[14] Ibid

[15] Ibid

[16] Ibid

[17] Ibid

[18] Ibid

[19] Ibid

[20] DiversityInc.com, "When 'Diversity Director' Means 'Dead End' - Malignant Neglect: Mistakes You Don't Know You're Making," by Linda Bean, January 15, 2002

[21] DiversityInc.com, "Corporate Culture: Check It Out Before You Take That Job," by Lee Anna Jackson, May 18, 2005

[22] Ibid

[23] Ibid

[24] Ibid

[25] DiversityInc.com, "Diversity 101: A Primer for Beginners," by Barbara Frankel, March 18, 2002

[26] Ibid

[27] *The Wall Street Journal*, "Pepsi, Vowing Diversity Isn't Just Image Polish, Seeks Inclusive Culture," by Chad Terhune, April 19, 2005

[28] Ibid

[29] Ibid

[30] Ibid

The leaders of well-managed companies know that the strong job growth that we've seen over the past few years, in addition to low unemployment, means that it's more critical than ever to attract the best talent as well as to retain and promote valuable employees. Strong diversity initiatives ensure that a company has the deepest pool of talent from which to draw while developing an environment where different employees are valued and respected, creating a more productive working environment for all employees.

WORK-FORCE DEMOGRAPHICS

Like marketplace demographics, work-force demographics constantly are evolving. As greater numbers of people of color, women, GLBTs and people with disabilities enter the work force, they represent a growing number of talented individuals who can provide firsthand insight into the marketplace and opportunities among their individual cultures. Similarly, people of color, women, gays, lesbians, individuals with disabilities and older workers each bring new perspectives and insights brought about by their own experiences.

CHAPTER 3

The People Side:

Cultivating
Human
Capital

DIVERSITY PROGRAMS AND YOUR EMPLOYEES

Whether your company currently has a strong diversity initiative or is in the process of becoming more inclusive, diversity initiatives directly affect your employees. Each employee will need to become more focused on creating a corporate environment that embraces differences. Employees must participate in training programs and cooperate with or participate in employee diversity councils. Comprehension of the value of diversity also often means changing the way employees are compensated, especially managers. The most progressive companies, including 88 percent of The 2005 DiversityInc Top 50 Companies for Diversity, directly tie managers' compensation to diversity success.

GETTING MANAGERS TO THINK INCLUSIVELY

One of the keys to fostering a strong corporate-diversity initiative is to ensure that management compensation is tied to diversity initiatives.

Corporate managers need to ensure that their staff reflects the company's commitment to diversity and that their outreach to external audiences—through sales, marketing, purchasing, customer service, production, or whatever areas they oversee—considers that not all audience members are the same.

Performance reviews, bonuses and raises should take into consideration a manager's adherence to and performance within corporate diversity directives.

In order for this to be effective, as we discussed in Chapter 2, it's essential that senior management be involved in ensuring that diversity initiatives are a priority within the company. When middle managers hear that their supervisors take diversity initiatives seriously and realize that their performance reviews will be affected by their adherence to those initiatives, the culture of a company begins to change at every level.

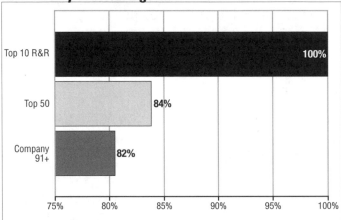

Diversity Training Mandatory for Managers?

Top 10 R&R — 100%
Top 50 — 84%
Company 91+ — 82%

Source: DiversityInc
*Top 10 Companies for Recruitment & Retention
Companies Ranked 91 and Higher on the 2005 Top 50 Survey

Training also is essential to getting managers to think more inclusively. All of the DiversityInc Top 10 Companies for Recruitment & Retention have mandatory diversity-training requirements for managers, compared with 80 percent of the Top 50, and 45 percent of the companies that ranked after 91.[1] It is essential that all employees be given at least basic diversity training, which should educate them about how to work effectively within a diverse culture. For managers, training should include showing how diversity directly impacts their areas of responsibility. For instance, marketing managers need to be trained in reaching out to diverse audiences as well as in how to recruit

Training also is essential to getting managers to think inclusively.

and cultivate diversity among the employees who report to them. More specific training information will be discussed in Chapter 4.

BOTTOM-LINE BENEFITS
OF A DIVERSE EMPLOYEE BASE

Creating this culture requires an investment of time and resources. But does it pay off?

Absolutely. Among the companies in The 2005 DiversityInc Top 50 Companies for Diversity list, the more inclusive the company, the higher its rate of employee retention in all groups. The retention rates for the DiversityInc Top 10 Companies for Recruitment & Retention are extremely high—between 91 percent and 94 percent—for everyone: whites, blacks, Asian Americans, Latinos and women. This shows they are connecting with all of their employees and, therefore, their customers, investors and suppliers as well.[2]

Retention: 2005 Top 50 Companies for Diversity

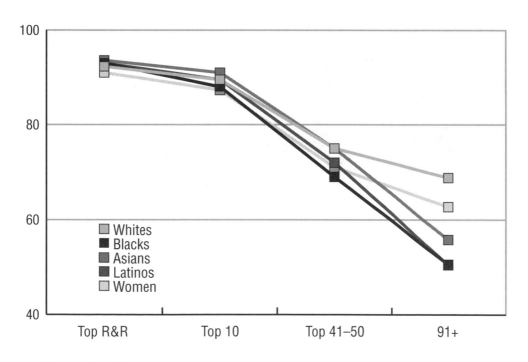

Source: DiversityInc

However, as we look at other groups of companies in The 2005 DiversityInc Top 50 Companies for Diversity survey—the Top 10, companies ranked 41–50, and companies ranked 91 plus—we see a growing racial/ ethnic gap. As the companies' rankings decline, the retention rates are lower for everyone but significantly lower for blacks and Latinos. The gap between blacks and Latinos is more than 20 percent when the Top 10 for Recruitment & Retention and the 91-plus companies are compared.[3]

...the more inclusive the company, the higher the rate of employee retention in all groups.

This shows a huge disconnect between these companies and their black and Latino employees. And if these companies aren't retaining black and Latino employees, they certainly aren't connecting with their black and Latino customers. Keep in mind as well that these are companies that voluntarily gave DiversityInc their data. Companies not participating in the survey would have far lower retention rates with people of color and women—and an even greater gap reaching their customers.[4]

When a company's diversity rating goes down, the differential between retention rates based on gender and race/ ethnicity increases proportionately. With an estimated replacement cost of $12,000 per employee, companies that retain their employees enjoy significant cost savings.[5]

The Employment Policy Foundation of the Society for Human Resources Management recently studied employee-turnover rates and found that the average

Does Your Company Have a Clear Statement on Diversity Goals and How They Fit Into Corporate Culture?

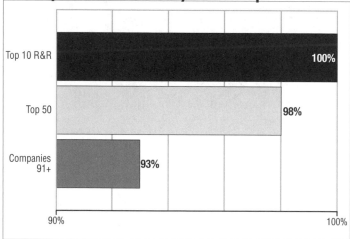

- Top 10 R&R: 100%
- Top 50: 98%
- Companies 91+: 93%

Source: DiversityInc
*Top 10 Companies for Recruitment & Retention
Companies Ranked 91 and Higher on the 2005 Top 50 Survey

annual rate for the 12 months ending August 2004 was 25.1 percent. Its estimates for total annual-turnover replacement costs further illustrate the need for inclusive corporate cultures that retain good employees. For large companies, differences in turnover rates can make large differences in costs—for a company with 40,000 full-time employees, the study estimates total turnover costs could reach $78 million annually with a 15 percent turnover rate. That is calculated on an estimated turnover cost of $13,000 per employee. With a 40 percent annual turnover rate, costs reached $214 million.[6] The study also found that the loss of productivity while a position is vacant and the diminished productivity

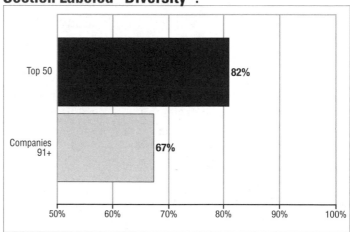

Source: DiversityInc
Companies Ranked 91 and Higher on the 2005 Top 50 Survey

during a new employee's transition period are significant aspects of the total cost of turnover. Companies that are able to reduce their turnover rate have a significant competitive advantage.[7]

CREATING A CULTURE OF DIVERSITY

We know that creating a diverse culture is important for recruiting and retaining employees. In addition, an inclusive culture can make a company more competitive and can save money on replacement costs. How can a company tell how well it's doing in creating that culture?

There are a number of criteria companies that are truly committed to diversity continually meet. Companies that are serious about their diversity initiatives generally make those efforts well known to both internal and external audiences. The following areas will provide telltale evidence of a company's level of commitment and all are part of the criteria of The 2005 DiversityInc Top 50 Companies for Diversity competition.

Web Sites. Many companies use this communication vehicle to proudly let the world know about their diversity efforts. When evaluating a site, look for details on work-force diversity, supplier diversity and community commitment. Examine photographs on the Web site and see whether the representation of people on the site is inclusive. Look for diversity awards and recognition, such as being included in The 2005 DiversityInc Top 50 Companies for Diversity list. Note how close this information is to the company's homepage; if it's featured prominently, that is a strong indicator that the company is proud of its diversity success.[8]

For example, anyone interested in pursuing a career with Bausch & Lomb (B&L) won't have much guesswork when it comes to figuring out what role diversity plays within the corporate culture at the eye-care-product manufacturer's offices, headquartered in Rochester, N.Y.

And that's the point. A visit to the careers section of its Web site emphasizes the seven cultural drivers that everyone up and down the ranks at B&L (No. 33 on The 2005 DiversityInc Top 50 Companies for Diversity list) is expected to adhere to at all times, together with a well-defined statement emphasizing the company's commitment to diversity.[9]

> **Companies serious about diversity will be clear about expectations.**

Research and a Clear Plan. Has your company put time and resources into planning its diversity initiatives? Is there a chief diversity officer or diversity director who reports to the CEO or at least to senior management? Are expectations about inclusiveness and corporate culture clearly communicated to employees?

If the answer to these questions is "yes," the company is likely doing a good job of creating a diverse culture. One example of doing things the right way was the merger between First Union and Wachovia (No. 31 on The 2005 DiversityInc Top 50 Companies for Diversity list) in September 2001. During the transition, leadership made a concerted effort to ensure that their culture would be well-defined. First, they administered a culture survey across the employee base of both organizations, approximately 90,000 people, and got close to a 60 percent response rate. They also commissioned the Gallup Organization to gauge their customer service.[10]

Even when information was shared with Wachovia's employee base about the brand's way to deliver service, the potential differential impacts across the different groups were evaluated to see what effects they could have on various identity groups.

Clear Communication. When a company indicates in its recruitment efforts or corporate communication that it wants to "access new markets" or hire people from "different backgrounds," it's a good sign that corporate leaders understand the need for different perspectives and talents for the company to flourish.[11]

In addition, companies serious about diversity will be clear about expectations, using written and verbal communication during the interview process, as well as diversity councils and written policies and procedures to ensure that employees are clear about the company's expectations.

To ensure that Wachovia's employees display the values and embrace the culture, a Service Excellence Group that utilizes various communication vehicles keeps employees abreast on the standard way to do everything from answering the phones to conducting business meetings. Each employee also has a wallet card that spells out the company's vision, value, brand and service philosophy, which serves as an everyday reminder of the corporate culture of diversity.[12]

Measurement. Companies that evaluate their employees and have metrics in place usually are right on track. For example, B&L employees meet with their managers twice a year to go through a guided process of identifying their developmental needs and having them addressed. The company's Performance Management System identifies the employee's strengths and weaknesses by measuring how he or she is meeting objectives. This process

> If you are working in a company that's "renovating" its philosophies, understand you may be held to a higher standard.

requires that objectives be set at the beginning of the year, and employee performance is to be measured mid-year and again six months later. If there are performance-related issues that need addressing, the Individual Development Planning Process allows employees to seek methods of resolution.[13]

Flexibility Toward Change. One key element helping employees adapt to diversity issues and the general ins and outs of corporate culture requires being receptive to change. If you are working in a company that's "renovating" its philosophies, understand you may be held to a higher standard.

Wal-Mart is just such an example. DiversityInc chronicled Wal-Mart's troubles with headlines such as "Baloney Meter: Wal-Mart's Empty Diversity Promises" and "Wal-Mart's Diversity Head Can't Back Claims with Numbers." Yet the company made The DiversityInc Top 50 Companies for Diversity list at No. 29 in 2005.[14]

Wal-Mart began to attack its diversity issues when it launched a diversity department in 2003. The department, which now employs about 100 people, has made progress in focusing on recruiting women, people of color, GLBTs and people with disabilities as well as retaining and marketing to consumers that they represent. From making new ties between management compensation and diversity, to finding opportunities for diverse suppliers, the company has vastly changed its approach to diversity.[15]

However, even in the face of such significant changes, the company still has diversity-related challenges that it must face. The company is facing a large class-action gender-discrimination suit, which the company is seeking to decertify. In March, the government dropped charges that the company hired undocumented workers. And Wal-Mart supporters and critics continue to debate the company's effect on small merchants in communities across the country. As of 2005, the company was spending only spending 2 percent of its procurement budget with diverse businesses.[16]

> **From making new ties between compensation and diversity, to finding opportunities for diverse suppliers, the company has vastly changed its approach to diversity.**

So, even though the company has made great strides in becoming more diverse, it still has work to do.[17]

It's been 10 years since Health Care Service Corp. (HCSC, No. 17 on The 2005 DiversityInc Top 50 Companies for Diversity list) formally created a diversity department after recognizing the positive business implications. The non-investor-owned mutual-insurance company based in Chicago, which operates through its Blue Cross/Blue Shield divisions in Texas, New Mexico and Illinois, found that when diversity is truly working, the organization actively understands cultural differences in the workplace as well as the market-

To make a diversity program work, individuality needs to be respected and welcomed.

place. While HCSC was in the process of overseeing a merger between two companies with different cultures—southwestern and Midwestern—the need to be responsive to cultural differences and develop a diversity strategy became even more obvious.[18]

Internally, HCSC managers are expected to take ownership of the company's diversity efforts and come up with a plan for how this will be integrated into every aspect of the way their business units do business. Their plans are reviewed every year and they are evaluated by the president. This accounts for 5 percent of the divisional bonus.[19]

This plan also must facilitate a better understanding of customers, including listening beyond accents and dialects and even understanding multicultural usage of various terms. For instance, in the South, blacks commonly refer to having 'sugar,' meaning diabetes. Understanding that simple language difference can mean communicating more effectively with a particular audience.[20]

LEADERSHIP INVOLVEMENT. All of a company's leadership needs to play a major role in setting the tone of a diversity program. As we discussed extensively in Chapter 2, it's critical that senior management play a key role in diversity initiatives.

ATTITUDE TOWARD INDIVIDUALITY. To make a diversity program work, individuality needs to be respected and welcomed. While employees and managers need to be given guidance on policies and procedures, there also has to be some latitude for employees to accomplish their goals within their own capabilities and strengths. Recognition of individual strengths and contributions is essential to creating a more inclusive culture.[21]

RECRUITMENT THAT WORKS. Fostering a diverse employee base begins with recruiting a diverse mix of employees. Recruitment is critical to having a diverse work force and having multicultural leaders of an organization. This, in turn, attracts multicultural consumers.

The first step to creating a multicultural and multifaceted work force can be as simple as declaring an intention to do so. Word of mouth can be a powerful tool in attracting diverse talent and companies that have a pro-diversity reputation. Whether it's a company known as an employer of choice for people of color, women, individuals with disabilities, gays and lesbians, or older workers, it will find a greater pool of applicants than those that do not enjoy the same reputation.

Partnering With Business Organizations. By developing relationships with business organizations that have ties to various demographic segments, companies can tap into those networks to attract talent. There are regional and national organizations that focus on Latinos, blacks and other racial and ethnic groups in business. For a list of these organizations, refer to the appendix.

> Companies should have clear information about their diversity initiatives on their Web sites, as well as information about how applicants may contact the company.

Recruiting on College Campuses. By targeting college campuses that have very diverse student populations, organizations can recruit the best talent right out of school. Contact colleges and universities and find out their percentage of black, Latino, Native American, Asian-American and white students. When the numbers are strongly multicultural, it's likely that you'll find candidates who will be attracted to

Diversity Leader: ALTRIA

Altria, the company ranked No. 1 on The 2005 DiversityInc Top 50 Companies for Diversity list, is the parent company of Philip Morris USA and Kraft Foods (No. 10 on The DiversityInc Top 50 Companies for Diversity list). Altria has a multi-tiered recruitment and retention strategy. Its commitment to constantly recruiting diverse candidates means that it has allowed it to develop a diverse senior-management team as well as a deep bench. Of Altria's new hires, 31 percent were people of color—13.25 percent black, 9 percent Asian American and 9 percent Latino.[23]

Altria has benefited from years of recruiting people of color at colleges and universities as well as among professional organizations.[24] Altria's CEO, Louis Camilleri, personally reviews diversity metrics and programs, and

an equally multicultural workplace. For a list of these organizations, refer to the appendix.

Tapping Employees, Affinity Groups and Employee Councils. Your own staff may be an excellent resource for recruiting diverse employees. By looking for recommendations from employees whose work is admired and whose reputation is trusted, companies can tap into a variety of networks to expand their reach into niche communities.

Publicizing the Company's Commitment to Diversity. As we have said before, companies that do a good job of communicating their commitment to diversity will attract candidates who wish to work in an inclusive culture. Companies should have clear information about their diversity initiatives on their Web sites, as well as information about how applicants may contact the company. A commitment to diversity should be expressed in the company's external communications, as well as in the corporate mission statement.

Advertising on Web Sites. The Internet is a powerful tool for recruiting diverse employees. Advertising on sites or in other media that are specifically targeted toward multicultural applicants, as well as the GLBT community, individuals with disabilities and older workers, is an excellent way to reach a wide pool of diverse applicants while promoting the company's own commitment to an inclusive culture. By using Web sites aimed specifically at diverse professionals, employers can advertise directly on a vehicle that is actively promoted to people of color, women, GLBTs and people with disabilities. Job applicants find companies that actively welcome them.[22]

signs off on management compensation tied to diversity, setting the tone for Altria's leaders who are expected to create environments that invite people to contribute.[25]

And it's working. Many departments conduct organizational reviews where directors share progress reports. This opens up the evaluation process so peer directors, in addition to managers, can say who is performing well.[26] All employees are required to go through diversity training.[27]

Altria's senior director, leadership development & diversity, Edith Chen, says that Altria's retention numbers are high because of the culture the company has built. Acceptance and respect for diverse points of view are essential for recruitment and retention success, she says.[28]

"People stay because they see opportunity. They have to know that those opportunities are gotten fairly and apply to everyone," she explains.[29]

Hosting Career Fairs or Networking Events. Introducing your company in a face-to-face setting can be a very effective tool for applicants to see the results of your company's diversity initiatives firsthand.

SPOTTING EFFECTIVE–AND MEANINGLESS–ONLINE RECRUITING SOLUTIONS

Diversity job boards, such as DiversityInc's Career Center, www.DiversityInc.com/Careers, are excellent vehicles to reach a talented, diverse pool of applicants. However, there are other online recruitment boards that generate little traffic and are nothing more than portals to larger, mass-market sites or, worse, a thin collection of low-potential jobs.

A good diversity job board not only will post jobs from companies that are looking to recruit diverse individuals—people of color, women, people with disabilities, GLBTs and older workers—but also will communicate to the company seeking employees what is important to this group. This may include information that should be included to make a job description more effective, such as:

A proper title and job description
Clearly stated employee benefits
Information about the company and its history
A clear statement about the company's commitment to diversity

This may make the company's copy longer than that of a traditional online recruitment ad, but job boards that value diversity will not charge the company exorbitant amounts of money to include this information.

Managers of effective boards understand that they need to be a bridge between the company and candidates. They should be able to give advertisers feedback on their ads because they should be monitoring response rates and traffic for various companies represented on the board and evaluating which ads are most effective.

In addition, the job board also should educate the applicant pool about matters related to their job search. Content on the best sites for diverse recruitment may include stories about workplace issues, résumé basics, creating a professional image, track records of inclusive companies, and other professional-development issues.

42

In addition, good job boards invest in technology that makes the board easy to navigate. However, clean graphics should not be the only litmus test for an effective diversity job board. It's possible that a great-looking site is merely a meaningless portal created by a larger job-data bank attempting to capitalize on the talent attracted to diverse companies. Some of the more recognizable online career centers simply create an interface that touts their commitment to diversity but do nothing more than link to jobs and companies that are targeted toward main-stream audiences. Some red flags that may indicate a job board does not truly have a commitment to diversity include:

It does not state its commitment to diversity clearly on the site.
It does not allow applicants to cloak their identities.
It just links to larger, mass-market job boards.
It does not have an employer-profile section. Diverse applicants want to know about a company's history to use as a launching point from which they can do further research on their own.

Be concerned if the board cannot provide percentages of people of color, women, GLBTs, individuals with disabilities and other audience segments who visit the site. A board that has the ability to disclose this aggregate information has developed a relationship with its candidates and they willingly share this information. This indicates that the board is well-run and cares about fostering relationships with its users—and shows that the audience trusts it.

RETAINING THE BEST

While recruitment is one part of the cultural-diversity equation, retention is even more critical. Corporations that have successfully recruited top diverse talent are frequently faced with the additional challenge of retaining these valuable and highly sought-after employees. Stellar multicultural employees bring insight and access to emerging markets that might otherwise be inaccessible to most corporations.

Once you've recruited employees of different races, ethnicities, cultural orientation, abilities, ages and genders, it's critical to take steps to ensure that the company is doing what it can to retain those individuals. While companies often think of losing employees to other companies, it's also common for people of color and women, especially, to join the ranks of entrepreneurs and start their own businesses.

How can you keep more of your best talent? The Top 10 Companies for Recruitment & Retention have higher retention rates in all categories of employees. Some of the best practices they use include:

MENTORING

In today's competitive business environment, employees need the voice of experience to show them the best career path. Companies on The 2005 DiversityInc Top 50 Companies for Diversity list have provided just such a lifeline to employees who need support. That lifeline is in the form of mentoring programs, allowing both new and established employees to avail themselves of the experience, wisdom and guidance of long-tenured staffers within their respective companies.[30]

And while it's a valuable service for anyone, it's particularly useful for people of color, women, GLBT employees and employees with disabilities, who often don't know how to negotiate in a culture so long dominated (and with the rules set) by white men.

Steve Reinemund, CEO of PepsiCo (No. 4 on The 2005 DiversityInc Top 50 Companies for Diversity list), knew the value of mentoring, which he described in an interview with *The Wall Street Journal*. Eight members of senior management were each named "executive sponsor" for a company-wide employee group, including blacks, Latinos, Asian Americans, women, white males, people with disabilities, and gay, lesbian, bisexual and transgender people.[31]

Citigroup: A Recruitment-and-Retention Success Story

The senior management at Citigroup (No. 3 on The 2005 DiversityInc Top 50 Companies for Diversity list and No. 8 on the 2005 Top 10 Companies for Recruitment & Retention list), the world's largest financial-services firm, takes its diversity initiatives so seriously that the diversity department routinely is included in discussions surrounding affinity marketing, procurement, corporate communications and employment law. In addition, this department also has responsibility for the company Web site.[59]

Recruitment and retention are two imperatives that led the company, which has 300,000 employees worldwide, to increase its understanding of the power of diversity. It worked. Between 2002 and 2004, the company's total representation of people of color grew from 28.4 percent to 33.4 percent in 2004, which Ana Duarte-McCarthy, Citigroup's director of global workforce diversity, credits largely to recruitment efforts.[60]

New hires in 2004 at Citigroup included 44 percent people of color—17.25 percent

The executives were placed with groups different from themselves. For instance, Irene Rosenfeld, CEO of Frito-Lay of North America, is white and the sponsor of the Latino group. Pepsi General Counsel Larry Thompson, who is black, oversees white men. It is the executives' responsibility to understand their members' needs, identify key talent and personally mentor three people in their group.[32]

Thompson told the *The Wall Street Journal* that one issue quickly emerged involving his group. "There is the assumption that white males have to be the loser in diversity programs and white men won't be champions of this," he says. But, he adds, "That is a false impression."[33]

Such programs allow seasoned employees to share their vast knowledge with newer employees. However, they also allow the veterans to learn from new voices with new perspectives.

BENEFITS

Do your benefits reflect the needs of your employee base? An examination of The 2005 DiversityInc Top 50 Companies for Diversity offers models of how employers are able to attract new talent and retain valued employees with lifestyle benefits while containing cost.[34]

WORK/LIFE BENEFITS

Companies on The 2005 DiversityInc Top 50 Companies for Diversity list have substantial work-at-home and/or telecommuting policies. One hundred percent offer work/life benefits, including the ability to work

black, 10.25 percent Asian American, 13 percent Latino—and 55 percent were women. Of the company's managers in 2004, 22 percent were people of color (8.25 percent black, 6 percent Asian American, 7.75 percent Latino) and 47 percent were women. The company also actively recruits for GLBTs and people with disabilities. The company has bolstered its diversity-recruitment efforts by participating on a number of Web sites, especially www.DiversityInc.com/Careers, and also engaging its 21 employee networks in recruiting. Each year, the company also looks for diverse candidates on college campuses.[61]

Retention also is a focus at Citigroup, and among the methods used to retain employees is mandatory diversity training for the company's approximately 3,000 managers. Diversity training also extends down to new hires and new managers at their orientation.[62]

Beyond diversity training, Citigroup uses its 21 employee networks to engage its employees both internally in developing programs and externally in their communities. Since 2002, when the network program was launched, these groups have become central to the company's most senior leaders, many of whom are sponsors of the networks.[63]

at home, flexible hours and job sharing. One hundred percent offer dependent-care benefits, including childcare and eldercare. In addition, all of the companies on The DiversityInc Top 50 Companies for Diversity list offer domestic-partner benefits for same-sex partners, and 88 percent offer adoption assistance.

The 2005 DiversityInc Top 10 Companies for Executive Women have more than 200 times the number of companies offering onsite child-care as corporate America on the whole (70 percent vs. 3 percent), almost twice as many as the rest of the 2005 Top 50 (39 percent) and almost three times as many as companies ranked higher than 91 on the 2005 Top 50 list (28 percent).[35]

These offerings are critical to retaining employees. While many employers are looking for ways to cut costs, they also take on programs that result in big savings. Sherry Wilson, director of the Employee Assistance and Work-Life programs at the University of Texas Health Science Center at Houston, says a worker typically loses 17 hours of work on average when he or she needs to look for a daycare provider. A referral program costing a few thousand dollars "can save the employer thousands of dollars a year keeping the employee on the job."[36]

A way to measure cost savings for work/life benefits is by considering the rate of absenteeism and turnover. Wilson cites a 1998 study by Work/Family Directions that showed for every $1 an employer spends in helping employees balance their home and work lives, the company will get a return investment of $3 to $4 in work hours saved, insurance costs, sick leave, decreased absenteeism and fewer on-the-job injuries.[37]

Employees also are less likely to put up with employers who don't respect their lives outside of work. Major benefits such as healthcare and retirement-saving plans are crucial, but neglecting "balancing benefits" will result in turnover. She cites childcare and eldercare as the two biggest areas where employees want flexibility.[38]

By 2007, 54 percent of Americans are expected to take care of an elderly parent, according to a 1997 study by the National Council on Aging, National Alliance for Caregiving and the AARP. The same study found that one in three employees still had children younger than 18 at home.[39]

Companies that offer attractive vacation benefits also score points with recruits and retain valued workers, according to a MetLife survey. MetLife is No. 36 on The 2005 DiversityInc Top 50 Companies for Diversity. Although 59 percent of employees surveyed worried about having sufficient health insurance and 49 percent worried about their retirement savings running out, 64 percent of full-time employees placed a higher value on vacation days than employer-funded pension plans, disability insurance, life insurance and long-term-care insurance.[40]

PricewaterhouseCoopers, one of the 2005 DiversityInc 25 Noteworthy Companies for Diversity, has been ahead of corporate America on work/life issues. The company's lactation program subsidizes nearly all of the cost of a $250 to $300 breast pump for female employees and the wives of male employees. The program not only helps ensure that valued employees stay with the company, but it directly affects many of the company's employees, whose average age is 32. The biggest medical expense is maternity care, as one-third of medical claims deal with maternity and childbirth.[41]

> **"There is the assumption that white males have to be the loser in diversity programs and white men won't be champions of this, but that is a false impression."** – Larry Thompson, PepsiCo

PricewaterhouseCoopers started its lactation program when an employee who gave birth to premature twins in the mid-1990s told of her difficulty pumping breast milk in the workplace and balancing her work life with her new responsibilities as a mother.[42]

For many companies, including Xerox (No. 7 on The 2005 DiversityInc Top 50 Companies for Diversity list), childcare is the most popular work/life benefit. The Xerox childcare subsidy is part of the company's LifeCycle Assistance Program, which allows employees to be reimbursed up to $10,000 over their careers at Xerox. Employees who earn up to $75,000 annually can get reimbursed for $2,000 a year to cover childcare costs until they reach the $10,000 limit. A 2004 benefits study by SHRM showed that top companies such as Xerox are the exception, as only 4 percent of the 457 surveyed companies subsidized childcare.[43]

HEALTHCARE BENEFITS

Healthcare benefits are the biggest cost for employers and employees yet are one of the most important benefits that employees require. Healthcare premiums for family coverage are moving toward an average of $12,000 a year and higher, according to a June 2004 Health Care Survey Report by SHRM. For an employee earning $40,000 a year, that represents almost 30 percent of his or her base salary and that is before other mandatory deductions, such as federal and state taxes, unemployment and workers'-compensation insurance.[44]

About 25 percent of the 373 companies surveyed in the SHRM survey cited the cost of mandatory health benefits as a higher percentage of salaries than a year earlier.[45]

Although both employee and employer contributions for healthcare have increased dramatically in recent years, employers of choice won't drop coverage altogether and seek out innovative ways to prevent health problems and to help their employees cover their costs. The work force is both shrinking and aging, meaning healthcare benefits increasingly are a competitive factor and the cost of healthcare for aging workers is skyrocketing. Corporations also are facing a dilemma about guaranteeing or subsidizing healthcare costs for retirees, many of whom live for several decades after leaving the company.[46]

For many companies, childcare is the most popular work/life benefit.

A shrinking labor force means that by 2010, workers ages 25 to 54 will increase by 1.2 percent, while those 55 to 64 will grow by 47 percent, according to the U.S. Bureau of Labor Statistics. About 48 million GenXers will be filling a labor hole left by 76 million baby boomers, creating a very competitive market for the best talent.[47]

From 2000 to 2004, corporate America dealt with double-digit healthcare-cost increases, from 12 percent to 16 percent on average, according to Leonard Sanicola, practice leader, professional development for WorldatWork, a nonprofit professional association that examines compensation, benefits and total-rewards issues.[48]

Sanicola sees a slight decrease in healthcare costs for 2005, between 8 percent and 10 percent, mainly because of cost controls from wellness and disease-control programs and a bottoming out of premiums. But he says health costs still outpace increases in inflation, 2 percent to 3 percent, and increases in wages, less than 3 percent on average, during the same period. This is one reason more employers have abandoned the once-popular health-maintenance organizations (HMO), which shielded employees from understanding their true health costs.[49]

A survey of more than 450 companies in the SHRM Benefits Survey showed 90 percent offered employees a preferred provider organization (PPO) in 2004, up from 82 percent in 2000. In contrast, the number of companies offering health-maintenance organization (HMO) plans dropped from 60 percent in 2000 to 51 percent in

Innovative ways companies have tried to contain costs include offering employees flexible-spending accounts.

2004. An HMO requires employees to pay a small amount when they visit a doctor, but it does not allow them to visit doctors outside their network. A PPO allows the employee a wider choice of services, but they must pay more outside their network.[50]

Innovative ways companies have tried to contain costs include offering employees flexible-spending accounts. These plans are similar to 401(k)s in that employees can contribute a set amount of pre-tax dollars to the account. Unlike a 401(k), the employee must use up the entire account in a year or lose the contribution. An employee can use the account to pay for a variety of expenses, including doctor-visit co-pays and prescriptions. Last year, the Internal Revenue Service broadened the allowable expenses to include over-the-counter and other health-related pharmacy purchases.[51]

The two most popular healthcare cost-management savings cited by human-resources managers surveyed by SHRM are having employees use a mail-order prescription program (78 percent of companies) and having employees share on premiums, co-pays and co-insurance (73 percent of companies).[52]

One newer option for cutting healthcare costs that companies are increasingly adopting are health savings accounts, which were signed into law by President Bush in December 2003.[53] These accounts are funded with pre-tax dollars similar to 401(k) plans and then used to pay medical expenses, often with a high deductible.[54] Paul Fronstin, director of health research and education program at the nonprofit Employee Benefit Research Institute (EBRI), believes 2006 will be a turning point for these accounts. Many employers operate on an annual cycle and, since the packages are relatively new, they did not have an opportunity to put them in place for 2005. However, he expects wider adoption by companies looking to reduce healthcare costs, especially if the Bush administration's plans for tax incentives for offering and participating in health-saving and health-retirement accounts come to fruition.[55]

DOMESTIC-PARTNER BENEFITS

Corporate America is leading the way with offering domestic-partner benefits for same-sex couples. All of The 2005 DiversityInc Top 50 Companies for Diversity offer domestic-partner benefits. In its report, The State of the Workplace for Lesbian, Gay, Bisexual and Transgender Americans 2004, the gay-rights group the Human Rights Campaign (HRC) found that the closer a company is to the top of the Fortune 500, the more likely it is to offer inclusive policies related to sexual orientation—all but one of the Fortune 50 includes sexual orientation in their nondiscrimination policies. HRC counted 8,250 employers that provided domestic-partner benefits to same-sex couples as of 2004, which is a 13 percent increase over the year before.[56]

STRONG EMPLOYEE NETWORKS

Employee-affinity groups and networks are important to fostering talent within a company and creating a connection with a corporate culture that's more than just a job. For example, Abbott Laboratories (No. 5 on The 2005 DiversityInc Top 50 Companies for Diversity list and No. 3 on the Top 10 Companies for Recruitment & Retention) has six employee-resource groups, including groups for women, blacks and part-time workers. These groups focus on career development, mentoring and networking. In addition to nurturing employee growth, these groups provide insight into the needs and concerns of the company's various constituencies and offer feedback on business strategies, such as those on product marketing. For example, Abbott's Latino-employee network was heavily involved in the development and promotion of Glucerna, a meal-replacement drink for people with diabetes.[57] Clearly, solid retention strategies not only are ensuring that employees remain with their employers for longer periods of time, but they are paying off in solid business results, including new product development, insight into emerging markets and positive word of mouth about the companies who offer them. In an economy where good employees are the most valuable commodity a company can have, the importance of investments in inclusive recruitment and retention can't be overstated. In 2003, Ford's 12 employee-resource groups added $80 million in vehicle sales to the company's coffers through the Ford Friends and Neighbors sales program.[58]

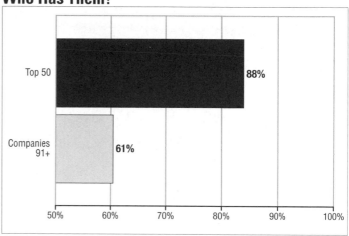

Employee-Resource Groups: Who Has Them?

Top 50: 88%
Companies 91+: 61%

Source: DiversityInc
Companies Ranked 91 and Higher on the 2005 Top 50 Survey

[1] *DiversityInc*, "Top 50 Companies for Diversity: Specialty Lists: Top 10 Companies for Recruitment and Retention," June 2005, page 74

[2] *DiversityInc*, "Diversity Trends," July/August 2005, page 22

[3] Ibid

[4] Ibid

[5] Compiled from The 2005 DiversityInc Top 50 Companies for Diversity

[6] Employment Policy Foundation, Society for Human Resources Management

[7] Ibid

[8] DiversityInc.com, "Corporate Culture: Check It Out Before You Take That Job," by Lee Anna Jackson, May 18, 2005

[9] Ibid

[10] Ibid

[11] Ibid

[12] Ibid

[13] Ibid

[14] *DiversityInc*, "The Top 50 Companies for Diversity List," June 2005, page 124

[15] Ibid

[16] Ibid

[17] Ibid

[18] DiversityInc.com,

"Corporate Culture: Check It Out Before You Take That Job," by Lee Anna Jackson, May 18, 2005

[19] Ibid

[20] Ibid

[21] Ibid

[22] DiversityInc.com, "Want to Find a Job? Use Web Sites, Networks and Events," by Yoji Cole, October 20, 2003

[23] *DiversityInc*, "Top 50 Companies for Diversity," June 2005, page 92

[24] Interview with Edith Chen, June 2005

[25] Ibid

[26] Ibid

[27] Ibid

[28] Ibid

[29] Ibid

[30] DiversityInc.com, "Need Help Moving Up or Finding Job Satisfaction? Try a Mentor," by Eric Hinton, May 18, 2005

[31] *The Wall Street Journal*, "Pepsi, Vowing Diversity Isn't Just Image Polish, Seeks Inclusive Culture," by Chad Terhune, April 19, 2005

[32] Ibid

[33] Ibid

[34] DiversityInc.com, "The Benefits of Knowing Your Benefits - Part I" by Peter

more>>>

Ortiz, February 11, 2005

[35] Aggregate information from The DiversityInc Top 50 Companies for Diversity

[36] DiversityInc.com, "The Benefits of Knowing Your Benefits - Part I," by Peter Ortiz, February 11, 2005

[37] Ibid

[38] Ibid

[39] Ibid

[40] Ibid

[41] Ibid

[42] Ibid

[43] Ibid

[44] DiversityInc.com, "The Benefits of Knowing Your Benefits - Part II" by Peter Ortiz, February 14, 2005

[45] Ibid

[46] Ibid

[47] Ibid

[48] Ibid

[49] Ibid

[50] Ibid

[51] Ibid

[52] Ibid

[53] Small Business Administration, Health Savings Accounts, http://www.sba.gov/health-care/

[54] Ibid

[55] Interview with Paul Fronstin, EBRI, June 2005

[56] Human Rights Campaign Foundation, "The State of the Workplace for Lesbian, Gay, Bisexual and Transgender Americans 2004"

[57] DiversityInc, "The Top 50 Companies for Diversity," June 2005

[58] Ibid

[59] Ibid

[60] Ibid

[61] Ibid

[62] Ibid

[63] Ibid

A company's diversity initiatives should be evident in its communication efforts to both internal and external audiences. Companies that cultivate a reputation for being inclusive—including being vocal about their diversity initiatives—reap the benefits of attracting a broader range of employees and customers.

IT STARTS WITH A MISSION (STATEMENT)

Corporate mission statements seem simple on the surface, but they are an important clue as to how a company operates and what its core values are. A mission statement that articulates a company's commitment to diversity is the essential cornerstone of an effective external diversity-communication program. Given the increasing diversity of the American work force and the multicultural consumer base, companies that express a commitment to work-force, marketplace and supplier diversity will attract the most talented employees and gain loyal investors and customers.

CHAPTER 4

Spreading the Word:

Corporate
Communications

In the past, a typical corporate mission statement was brief, to the point and primarily addressed increasing shareholder value. Today, however, corporate America needs to address far more in its mission. After all, Enron and WorldCom both were committed to increasing shareholder value—even if the companies defined "shareholder" as a select group of people in the know.

A corporation should be using its mission statement to develop trust among its varied constituency of employees, customers and investors. Indeed, a company must communicate diversity in its mission to all of its corporate stakeholders, not just shareholders. That includes employees, customers, suppliers, community members and anyone who has an interest in or is affected by the company's operations and policies.

Companies can use their mission statement as an effective tool to build trust among their varied constituencies. Look for references to "inclusive," "diverse," and "nondiscrimination," as well as "integrity" and "trust," in addition to references to success and profits. Such language tells each audience segment that the company is committed to success while respecting people and adhering to its own values. Corporate leaders who lose that commitment, as we've seen from the many Wall Street scandals in recent years, too easily jeopardize their companies and all that is at stake for the people involved with that company.

EVALUATING YOUR OUTREACH

DiversityInc magazine and www.DiversityInc.com have a regular feature called "Scorecard." In this feature, we critique a company's Web site as a measure of its commitment to diversity, giving a point-based grade to the online presence of leading corporations. The eight criteria are:

- Is there a link to diversity or diversity-related information on the home page? (Value: 1 point)

Companies can use their mission statement as an effective tool to build trust among their varied constituencies.

- Is there a link to diversity or diversity-related information within one click from the home page? (Value: 1 point)
- Does the Web site have a search function, and does a simple search for the keyword "diversity" yield relevant results? (Value: 3 points)
- Is the diversity information up-to-date? (Value: 1 point)
- Does the site use multicultural images? (Value: 1 point)
- Does the site offer diversity information in its career area? (Value: 2 points)
- Does the site offer information for diverse suppliers? (Value: 1 point)
- Does the site highlight the activities that impact diverse communities? (Value: 2 points)

Companies that score 11 points get an 'A,' those with 8–10 points get a 'B,' 5–7 ranks a 'C,' 2–4 gets you a 'D,' and anything below is failing. [1]

These criteria can be adapted as a checklist for any corporate communications outreach, regardless of media. As you examine your corporate communications efforts, consider the following:

- Is there diversity or diversity-related information reflected in your outreach?
- Is there direction on how to get more information on your company's diversity policies?

- Is the diversity information reflected in your communications up-to-date?
- Does your company regularly use multicultural images in its outreach, including advertising, direct mail, in-store promotions and other vehicles?
- Do your corporate-communication efforts regularly highlight the activities in which your company engages which impact diverse communities?
- When you're reaching out to multicultural markets, do you tailor efforts to speak to them more effectively? For instance, do you translate communications targeted to Spanish-speaking audiences, or consider which messages would best appeal to particular audience segments?
- Does your corporate mission statement include references to "diversity," "inclusion," and/or "nondiscrimination," and is that mission frequently cited in communications outreach?
- Do internal communications efforts include information about diversity?
- Do company newsletters, intranets and other internal vehicles use images of diverse employees?
- Are diversity councils and diversity directors consulted for outreach to various audience segments, and do they give input on the needs of those audiences?

As you can see, launching an inclusive communications effort requires thought and strategy. Companies need to consider the various components of their promotional and informational strategies and audiences by segment. Messages addressing the concerns of internal audiences—employees, investors, partners, etc.—will be different than those of external audiences—customers, community members, etc. Tailoring your message appropriately will deliver bottom-line benefits, such as reaching customers in diverse emerging markets while increasing employee satisfaction and investor confidence, to name a few.

REACHING EXTERNAL AUDIENCES

Inclusive external communications can help companies reach the emerging markets we discussed in Chapter 1. With the population of people of color reaching all-time highs, in addition to more women earning more money, and GLBTs and people with disabilities controlling a sizeable amount of discretionary income, companies that are able to use their existing knowledge base to develop products, services and outreach to these markets will reap the benefits of having new, loyal long-term customers.

ADVERTISING

Foreign-language and lifestyle media, including publications, broadcasts and online vehicles that target Latinos, blacks, Asian Americans, Native Americans, peoples with disabilities and GLBT people, serve a wide range of emerging markets. Corporate marketers need to carefully examine their advertising budgets to determine whether it makes sense to incorporate these vehicles into their marketing strategies.

Messages addressing the concerns of internal audiences—employees, investors, partners—will be different than those of external audiences—customers, community members.

Companies that do this are reaping the rewards of loyal customers who appreciate feeling valued and recognized. When Toyota took over the top spot for the most popular brands of cars among Latinos in the first quarter of 2004, corporate leaders at Ford Motor Company (No. 11 on The 2005 DiversityInc Top 50 Companies for Diversity list) decided to take action. In 2004, Ford announced a multicultural marketing campaign to focus on Latinos, blacks, and Asian

The PR Industry's Little White Secret

When it comes to public relations, image is everything. Unfortunately, this industry's image (and reality) is overwhelmingly white and exclusive, according to a study by two professors and communications-management agency RF Binder Partners.[17]

Discrimination, lack of mentoring and little interest in diversity among industry executives are a few of the problems uncovered in the survey of 132 black, Latino and Asian-American PR professionals. There was a 10 percent response rate.[18]

The survey was conducted online in October 2004 and January 2005 by Lynn Appelbaum, chairperson of the Department of Media & Communication Arts at The City College of New York, and Rochelle Ford, assistant professor, advertising and PR-sequence coordinator at Howard University.[19]

Nearly 82 percent of the participants were women, which is representative of the industry's makeup, Appelbaum said. Three-quarters of respondents were black, about 23 percent were Latino and about 1 percent were Asian American—the survey's one deficit, according to Appelbaum. She said many Asian Americans weren't interested in completing yet another survey, although they did participate in pre- and post-survey discussion groups.[20]

About half of the respondents reported being treated unfairly in the workplace and 40 percent said they had experienced overt discrimination. The most common problem (reported by 62 percent of respondents) was the perception that people of color have to be more qualified for positions than their white counterparts. Additionally, 60 per-

Americans with individual ads for each group, promoting the 2005 Five Hundred and 2005 Freestyle.[2]

More companies are realizing that the GLBT audience is a loyal customer base. One survey found that nearly two-thirds of the GLBT audience is extremely or very likely to consider products and services from companies that market directly to them.[3] The result, in some cases, has been ads featuring happy same-sex couples. A 2004 report by market-research publisher Packaged Facts estimated the buying power of this group at $610 billion in 2005.[4]

Another component of making advertising efforts inclusive is the use of language. The Pew Hispanic Center reports that the majority of first-generation Latinos (72 percent) primarily speak Spanish. However, those numbers shift dramatically among second-generation Latinos, of whom only 7 percent primarily speak Spanish, and the remaining group is split among individuals who are bilingual and those who speak only English. By the third generation, no Latinos speak only Spanish and the vast majority—78 percent—speaks only English.

These statistics make a strong argument for investment in ethnic media if they are targeting unacculturated immigrants who have not

cent of those surveyed said practitioners of color are put on slow-moving career tracks.[21]

Because of these problems, it's not surprising that just 45.8 percent of the respondents said they were satisfied or very satisfied with their jobs. Latinos experience significantly lower levels of job satisfaction than blacks—2.67 on a scale of 1 to 5, compared with 3.45, respectively.[22]

Using survey data and comments made during the discussion groups, representatives from the company identified several key steps the industry should take. Diversity training for staff, including managers, is an obvious first step.[23]

Mentoring came up repeatedly during discussions. And people of color don't necessarily need to be matched with mentors who look like them; they just want to work with someone who is eager to share their knowledge.[24]

To increase diversity, firms should make human-resources staff accountable for recruitment and retention of people of color. They also should create partnerships with career-counseling offices at universities with diverse student populations and historically black colleges and universities. But the report advises firms not to create a quota system. "Forget about hir-

ing 'token minorities,'" it says. "Hire the best-qualified candidates, but seek out and be genuinely open to recruiting multicultural practitioners."[25]

Reluctant industry executives might complain that this survey focuses too much on perceptions, which aren't always true. That's fair, says Rochelle Ford, assistant professor, advertising and PR-sequence coordinator at Howard University, one of the survey chiefs. "But let's think about what we tell our clients," she added. "The perception is oftentimes stronger than ... the reality."[26]

yet adopted English as their primary language.[5]

Cultural sensitivity also is essential in advertising, especially if a campaign is targeted across demographic lines. For instance, because of language construction and cultural norms, some taglines, slogans and even product names don't lend themselves to direct translation.

Allstate: A Multicultural-Marketing Success Story

Allstate has made a concerted effort to reach the diverse groups within its consumer constituency. While the company keeps specific dollar amounts confidential, in 2004, 6 percent of the company's marketing budget was directed toward multicultural marketing. Seven percent of the company's media budget was allocated to ethnic media.[27]

In the past, Allstate has achieved great success marketing to ethnic audiences. In the early 1990s, Allstate decided to harness diversity as a business benefit, recruiting agents of color and targeting Latino consumers with in-language advertising and product offerings. From 1996 to 2001, Allstate spent $60 million marketing to Latino consumers and found its business among those consumers increased from $1 billion to more than $2.1 billion. Allstate has continued to aggressively pursue marketing with campaigns geared toward blacks, Latinos and Asian Americans. [28]

A good example is one from the California Milk Processor Board. Executive Director Jeff Manning admitted that a direct Spanish-language translation of the phrase "Got Milk?" was considered, but Latino marketing expert Anita Santiago, who helped develop the Spanish-language milk campaign, pointed out the poor translation, which referenced lactation, before the campaign hit the marketplace.[6]

More significantly, however, the board also learned in advance that the concept of the English-language campaign was completely inappropriate for a Latino audience. The concept of milk deprivation was an insult to traditional Spanish-speaking women, who take pride in providing for their families. Given the importance of food and family in Latino cultures, the board developed a campaign that tapped into that focus, featuring the Spanish-language tagline "Have you given them enough milk today?" After a few years, the board revised the campaign in order to reach beyond Latina moms. Current efforts feature the tagline "Familia, Amor, Leche" ("Family, Love, Milk").[7]

The company actually used this lesson in multicultural marketing to its advantage. Manning said the organization had hoped its "Got Milk?" translation story would have served as a lesson for other marketers developing cross-cultural communications.[8]

"We used it as a funny little way of showing how we didn't fall in the hole and it became a story about how we did fall in the hole," Manning said of media coverage of the campaign. "What was never reported was not using the milk-deprivation strategy. That actually would have been considerably more disastrous if we had chosen to go that way strategically."[9]

Advertising that does not take into account cultural nuances also can generate negative publicity. While Sandals Resorts International, which operates resorts in Jamaica, the Bahamas and other Caribbean countries, regularly advertises its couples-only policy, until recently, it did not allow gay or lesbian couples to stay at its properties. The Kingston, Jamaica–based company defined "couple" as one man and one woman. Gay and lesbian couples wishing to stay at Sandals have been referred to Beaches, Sandals' sister property, which welcomes families, singles and both opposite-sex and same-sex couples.[10]

...because of language construction and cultural norms, some taglines, slogans and even product names don't lend themselves to direct translation.

For the past 10 years, Sandals received the "Rock Bottom" award for its policy against same-sex couples from "Out & About," a gay-travel newsletter published by PlanetOut Partners. The award, which is part of the publication's annual editor's choice awards, was designed to encourage change among companies the publication feels treats gays and lesbians unfairly.[11] The resort reversed its policy on same-sex couples in August 2004.[12]

In addition to generating negative press, the resort also was missing out on business. According to a survey by Community Marketing (CMI), more than 70 percent of the GLBT respondents planned to spend at least $2,500 per person on travel within 12 months; 25 percent planned to spend at least $5,000 per person.[13]

Based on national population figures, the U.S. gay and lesbian community represents a nearly $60-billion travel market, or an estimated 10 percent of the nearly $600 billion the Travel Industry Association of America estimates will be spent on domestic and international travel in 2005.[14] But CMI finds that the loss is an even larger percentage of the overall travel market in terms of gay and lesbian dollars invested in travel. The company found that approximately 97 percent of GLBT travelers took a vacation within the past 12 months, compared with a national average of 64 percent. Fifteen percent of GLBT travelers booked trips to the Caribbean.[15]

PUBLIC RELATIONS

One miscommunication from an employee who is not skilled in handling media inquiries can render meaningless a CEO's eloquence on diversity issues. Customer-service departments that don't offer support options for customers who don't speak English can erase years of effective marketing.

Training in cultural competency is especially important for public-relations programs. Smart companies have averted potential embarrassment in the press by making sure that they put properly trained professionals who are knowledgeable about diversity in contact with reporters who have questions about diversity-related issues.

Strong diversity initiatives and their positive impact are great fodder for media stories and can be a terrific opportunity to work with various media to tell your company's story. The key to telling that story effectively is to ensure that your company is delivering that story in a consistent and unified manner. When a corporation spends millions per year on advertising and recruitment efforts, and usually has additional investments in corporate giving, employee relations and cause-related marketing, each expense represents an important area of focus. These cost centers are necessary to generate hundreds or thousands of messages aimed at consumers, investors, communities and other stakeholders.

But what if those hundreds of messages were inconsistent or, worse, contradictory? In multicultural markets, for example, contradictory messages can lead to distrust, and that can lead to loss of business. If your company tries to tout its diversity story to the media, and is then hit with a racial-bias suit from its employees, those efforts and expenditures will have backfired.

Therefore, public-relations strategies need to be well-planned and integrated. Plans should include clear definition of messages, and set specific goals in reaching out to diverse audiences. For instance, if your goal is to inform more Latinos of your inclusive policies in order to attract a broader applicant pool of Latinos, you need to examine the best way to reach that audience. You may need to cultivate relationships with Spanish-language media and hire a translator to submit bylined articles or news releases to that media. You may wish to consult your company's Latino affinity group to see what aspects of the company would appeal most to this group. It's essential to gather as much insight as possible into the group you are targeting.

Public-relations efforts also must be subject to measurement. Examine the effectiveness of your program in terms of both reach—the impressions generated through publicity, public speaking and related efforts—and outcomes. Did the effort generate more inquiries from Latino applicants? If so, it's a good sign that your public-relations efforts are effectively targeting diverse audiences.

Being part of The DiversityInc Top 50 Companies for Diversity list also is a good PR move. Increasingly, there is tangible evidence that national recognition based on evaluation by empirical data gives companies credibility with customers, current and future employees, suppliers, investors and the public at large. Companies use their ability to land on corporate "lists" such as The DiversityInc Top 50 Companies for Diversity, Fortune's 100 Best Companies to Work For and Working Mother's 100 Best Companies for Working Mothers to improve their image and gain traction with their stakeholders.[16]

DIRECT MARKETING/ COLLATERAL MATERIALS

Consider your target audience when you create collateral or direct-mail materials. If you're reaching out to a niche audience, the message, language and images should be tailored appropriately. If the brochure or mailing is going to be widely distributed, be sure that it reflects a rich tapestry of differences—images should be reflective of an inclusive culture and text should make references to the company's commitment to diversity, if appropriate. Again, what your company shows is as important as what it says.

FINDING MULTICULTURAL- MARKETING ASSISTANCE

Sometimes, the best way to design multicultural-marketing, public-relations or advertising campaigns is to call in experts who are versed in reaching your target audience segments. Today's emerging markets also have led to a new industry of multicultural- and specialty-marketing firms that focus on niche markets.

If you do decide to reach out for help, you still need to have an understanding of the type of help that you need. There are many marketing-services providers out there, fulfilling different functions. Choose the wrong one and you could lose a significant amount of money. Some of your options include:

Agencies: These generally are multiple-person firms that have an area of specialization that may include advertising, public relations, sales promotions, events and/or other marketing services. A "virtual agency" often is a group of freelancers that have grouped together to get bigger clients or provide a greater range of services. Often, the bigger the agency, the higher the fee. Big agencies have big overhead.

Studios: Studios generally focus on graphic design or other visual creative generation. They may be one person or more, and fees, again, often grow as the size of the studio grows.

Questions to Ask Multicultural-Marketing Providers

■ What is your background in reaching this market segment?

■ What projects have you handled that are similar to my needs?

■ What were the outcomes of those projects?

■ How long did it take to reach those outcomes?

■ How do you measure success of a project or program?

■ How do you charge/what is your rate?

■ What provisions are made if the project does not work out as planned?

■ How will you report activity and results to me?

■ Who will be doing the actual work on my account?

■ What happens if I'm not satisfied with that person's work?

■ May I have three or four (or more) references?

Consultants/Independent Contractors: These soloists usually provide a specialized service: advertising, design, public relations, direct mail, etc. However, they may have colleagues who can offer other services, if necessary. Consultant rates vary greatly depending on market, area of expertise, years of experience and other factors.

When a provider calls itself "full service," that generally means that most services are performed in-house. However, many firms call themselves full service when they actually subcontract a portion or even most of their offerings to other contractors. So it's important to ask questions about who will be doing the work on your project.

INTERNAL COMMUNICATIONS

Just as important as communicating to external audiences are the efforts directed toward a company's internal audiences. More than anything, these include employees but also may include contract workers and board members who are closely allied with the company.

There are a number of internal tools that corporations can use to reinforce diversity messages to employees. The following are among the most important.

DIVERSITY COUNCILS

Diversity councils can be powerful tools in harnessing the power of your employee base to further diversity initiatives within your organization. External diversity councils often include executives of color and women from both inside and outside the company, as well as members from organizations that represent the interests of people of color, GLBTs, people with disabilities and women. Diversity councils meet regularly to discuss and assist in implementing ideas that make a corporate culture more inclusive at every level.

Diversity councils work best when they are chaired by the CEO or COO. When the managers who are directly accountable for a company's profits and performance spend time on a committee or council, it sends a clear message to all that diversity is an imperative within the organization. At the same time, it allows the members of the diversity council to communicate directly with the highest levels of management within the organization, ensuring that their messages, concerns and ideas are heard clearly.

EMPLOYEE-RESOURCE GROUPS

Employee-resource groups, or affinity groups, are an important way for companies to gain employee support, test products and ideas targeted toward various sectors, and recruit new workers. Unlike diversity councils, these groups usually represent a single sector of the company, representing the concerns and contributions of, for example, employees who are black, Latino, Asian American, Native American, people with disabilities, women, or gay, lesbian, bisexual or transgender.

Among The 2005 DiversityInc Top 50 Companies for Diversity, 88 percent have employee-resource groups, versus 61 percent of companies ranked higher than 91 in the survey, and in 96 percent of the top 50 the company funds them, versus 81 percent of companies ranked higher than 91. In 95 percent of The 2005 DiversityInc Top 50 Companies for Diversity, a senior executive is a member of each of these groups versus 78 percent of companies ranked 91 plus.[31]

The groups provide support to business objectives through participation in a variety of areas. They may weigh in on benefits packages or internal policy decisions. In the case of PepsiCo, affinity groups helped contribute to adding 1 percent to the corporate bottom line by providing input on such products as guacamole-flavored Doritos and soft drinks aimed at black consumers.[32] In 91 percent of The 2005 DiversityInc Top 50 Companies for Diversity, these groups are used to augment recruiting efforts versus 78 percent of companies ranked 91 plus.[33]

Health Care Service Corp.: Diversity Councils in Action

A decade ago, Health Care Service Corp.'s (No. 17 on The 2005 DiversityInc Top 50 Companies for Diversity list) director of corporate diversity, Rita Taylor-Nash, and her boss, President and CEO Raymond McCaskey, wondered who would chair their company's first diversity council. When asked who among his senior staff would take the lead, he replied, "Why don't I do it?" Health Care Service Corp. (HCSC) is No. 17 on The 2005 DiversityInc Top 50 Companies for Diversity list.[29]

Company leaders credit the diversity council with raising awareness of diversity initiatives through all levels of the company. Taylor-Nash calls them "tentacles that went out into the organization for us."[30] Along with other strong diversity initiatives, the council has helped HCSC achieve leadership status in human-capital diversity.

Like diversity councils, however, employee-resource groups work best when there is a senior manager involved. Sometimes, the managers are members of the sector the affinity group represents—but not always. At Pepsi, each affinity group is "sponsored" by a representative who may not be like the group's constituents. The company's management believes that this fosters a greater understanding across demographic lines.[34]

INTERNAL VEHICLES

Today, companies use myriad internal vehicles to communicate to their employees. These may range from newsletters to group e-mail to employee handbooks to corporate intranets. Companies that are serious about diversity need to ensure that these vehicles are also reflecting the company's inclusive nature. Use the checklist found earlier in this chapter to determine whether these vehicles are regularly reporting on diversity issues. Do employee handbooks clearly reflect diversity policies, procedures and expectations? Do corporate intranets have information about affinity groups, and career management information? Are the images used in these vehicles consistent with the inclusive culture for which the company strives? Examine these vehicles to ensure that they are reflective of the company's commitment to diversity.

By ensuring that every internal communication adheres to the same diversity guidelines as external communication, employees will be reassured that the company's inclusive culture truly permeates its operations.

OPEN-DOOR AND FEEDBACK POLICIES

Employees need to have clear ways to communicate their needs and concerns to management. Companies should have written policies for employees to report their concerns about diversity, inclusion and other workplace issues. It's critical that employees feel as though their input is valued and that they are not at risk for any sort of retaliation.

Companies that manage their internal communications as scrupulously as their external communications will find a greater degree of employee trust. By ensuring that every internal communication adheres to the same diversity guidelines as external communication, employees will be reassured that the company's inclusive culture truly permeates its operations and isn't just a positive public-relations campaign designed for external audiences.

TRAINING

Training is essential to the success of a diversity program. Companies need to ensure employees are working from an existing base of knowledge about the organization's expectations when it comes to inclusivity.

All of The 2005 DiversityInc Top 50 Companies for Diversity offer diversity training, as opposed to 94 percent of companies ranked 90 or higher on the survey. Among the 2005 DiversityInc Top 10 Companies for Recruitment & Retention, diversity training is mandatory for managers, compared with 84 percent of the top 50 and 82 percent of companies ranked 91 plus.

However, beyond the basics, it's also essential to determine which personnel will need specialized training. Managers, especially those whose performance is tied to diversity initiatives, need to be trained in recruiting, cultivating and managing diverse employees. Sales and marketing teams may need to be trained in evaluating multicultural markets. Customer-service representatives may need to be trained in cultural competency so that they can effectively serve a wider variety of customers. Purchasing managers may need training to become more aware of seeking out and working with diverse suppliers.

As diversity initiatives permeate the company, it's likely that new areas for training may be found. Companies that are serious about their inclusive cultures dedicate resources for training to address these issues as they arise.

WHAT WORKS
IN DIVERSITY TRAINING

Training needs to support a company's specific initiatives. Programs should be followed up by discussion with supervisors, including how those lessons can be applied. Training also can be effective when it is conducted in small groups or when employees work in pairs to complete the training.

Frequency and availability of training also is critical. Seventy-eight percent of The 2005 DiversityInc Top 50 Companies for Diversity offer training monthly, while only 45 percent of companies ranked 91 or higher offered training at such intervals. Among the DiversityInc Top 10 Companies for Recruitment & Retention, 30 percent offer training for more than two days at a time, whereas only 23 percent of those companies in the Top 50 and a mere 4 percent of companies ranked 91 plus offered the same.

The key is accountability. Companies need to set measurable objectives for the training and then use tools—quizzes, follow-up sessions, or other forms of information gathering—to determine if the training produced those outcomes. If not, the program needs to be improved or the employee needs to do more work in that area.

WHAT DOESN'T WORK IN DIVERSITY TRAINING

One-shot training programs that are not supported by the company culture, managers and company resources will largely be a waste of time and money. Additionally, training within a culture that is not committed to diversity and that does not "walk its talk" through inclusive policies and programs will fail. Training needs to be mandatory for individuals at all levels of the organization. It needs to be accessible— held at regularly scheduled intervals, at least once a month. And it needs to be supported by a culture that is truly inclusive.

[1] *DiversityInc*, "Making the Grade," featured monthly in magazine's Scorecard department

[2] *DiversityInc*, "Who Will Capture Latino Auto Buyers? Foreign vs. Domestic Battle," by Peter Ortiz, December 2004/January 2005, page 104

[3] Harris Interactive online survey, released February 4, 2005. http://www. harrisinteractive.com/news /allnewsbydate.asp?News ID=889

[4] Packaged Facts, "The U.S. Gay and Lesbian Market." September 2004

[5] Report: "Hispanics: A People in Motion," 2005; Chart: Pew Hispanic Center/Kaiser Family Foundation National Survey of Latinos, December 2002

[6] DiversityInc.com, "The Truth About Marketing Urban Legends: Got Milk?, Gerber Baby Food, Chevy Nova," by Angela D. Johnson, January 12, 2004

[7] Ibid

[8] Ibid

[9] Ibid

[10] DiversityInc.com, "No Gay Honeymooners Welcome at This Resort," by Angela D. Johnson, March 09, 2004

[11] Ibid

[12] *USA Today*, "Same-sex Twosomes Now Welcome at Sandals," by Kitty Bean Yancey, 10/14/04 Confirmed in interview with Sandals representative Mike Hicks.

[13] DiversityInc.com, "No Gay Honeymooners Welcome at This Resort" Community Marketing, Inc., "CMI's Gay and Lesbian Travel Profile. http://www.community marketinginc.com/ demographics.cfm. http://www.diversityinc .com/members/6495.cfm

[14] Travel Industry Association of America, "TIA's Annual Forecast."

http://www.tia.org/Press/ pressrec.asp?Item=369

[15] Ibid

[16] *DiversityInc*, "Why Participate? Ask Employees, Customers, Vendors & Investors," by Angela Johnson Meadows, June 2005, page 38

[17] DiversityInc.com, "The PR Industry's Diversity Problem," By T.J. DeGroat, June 10, 2005

[18] Ibid

[19] Ibid

[20] Ibid

[21] Ibid

[22] Ibid

[23] Ibid

[24] Ibid

[25] Ibid

[26] Ibid

[27] *DiversityInc*, "Top 50 Companies for Diversity," June 2005, page 106

[28] DiversityInc.com, "After Success Marketing to Blacks & Latinos, Allstate

Courts Asian Americans," by Yoji Cole, September 22, 2003

[29] *DiversityInc*, "Top 50 Companies for Diversity," June 2005 page 116

[30] Ibid

[31] Aggregate data, the DiversityInc Top 50 Companies for Diversity list

[32] *The Wall Street Journal*, "Pepsi, Vowing Diversity Isn't Just Image Polish, Seeks Inclusive Culture," By Chad Terhune, April 19, 2005; Page B1

[33] Aggregate data, the DiversityInc Top 50 Companies for Diversity

[34] Ibid, *Wall Street Journal*

Supplier diversity means that your company purchases the goods and services it needs from a variety of businesses, including those owned by people of color, women and people with disabilities. Like affirmative action, supplier diversity started out as a government mandate and has evolved into a competitive advantage for forward-thinking companies. As corporate America continues to try to find ways to cut costs and faces increasing pressure to make inroads into the fast-growing racial and ethnic markets, supplier diversity has emerged as one of the most viable and measurable methods of accomplishing those goals. Suppliers owned by women, people of color, GLBTs and people with disabilities provide unique insights into emerging markets, build a loyal customer base and, most importantly, create wealth in communities.

The 2005 DiversityInc Top 10 Companies for Supplier Diversity spent an average of 11.6 percent of their procurement budgets with diverse suppliers. That's almost double the 6.8 percent average of companies on The DiversityInc Top 50 Companies for Diversity list, and almost six times the national average of 2 percent.[2]

SUPPLIER-DIVERSITY BASICS

Supplier diversity has been described as an enlightened business decision based on keen awareness of demographic changes in a competitive marketplace. The historic reality is that motives were somewhat less forward-thinking and more compliance-driven. Companies doing business with the federal government need to meet federally mandated supplier-diversity requirements. (See Opportunity in Action sidebar.)

CHAPTER 5

Supplier Diversity

The private sector's first organized foray into supplier diversity was the result of the Chicago Business Opportunity Fair of 1968. Brought about by the civil unrest following the assassination of the Rev. Martin Luther King Jr., the event was the work of three organizations: The Chicago Economic Development Corporation (CEDC), the Chicago Urban League, and the Western Electric Company. The CEDC later would become the Chicago Minority Business Development Council (CMBDC) and would inspire the founding of the National Minority

Supplier Diversity Council (NMSDC).

Since those early days, competitive businesses have expanded their supplier-diversity programs, with telecommunications and auto companies having long been supplier-diversity leaders, making up the bulk of the Billion Dollar Roundtable (companies that spend $1 billion or more a year with WBEs and MBEs). The leadership of these industries is demonstrated by Ford Motor Co.'s (No. 11 on The 2005 DiversityInc Top 50 Companies for Diversity list) Web-based supplier-diversity reporting system, M-Tier, which allows the automaker to determine whether all of its vendors are spending money with people of color.[4]

The historic reality is that motives were somewhat less forward-thinking and more compliance-driven.

M-Tier, which stands for Multiple Tier Reporting, allows Ford to expand its oversight throughout the supplier chain to identify suppliers who aren't working with minority-owned businesses. The system tracks supplier spending to the fourth level of subcontracting, where it is often dealing with very small businesses.

The company has a longstanding commitment to forging relationships with businesses owned by people of color. Ford spent more than $3.7

Opportunity in Action: Federal Supplier-Diversity Requirements

Companies that are doing business with the federal government must adhere to several laws regarding subcontracting to small business, including Section 8(d) of the Small Business Act, Public Law 95-507, Public Law 103-355 and FAR 19.702. These laws require prime contractors having contracts that exceed the simplified acquisition threshold (more than $100,000) to provide maximum practicable subcontracting opportunities to small businesses, HUBZone small businesses, small disadvantaged businesses, and women-owned small businesses.

These laws, among other things, require that:

"On contracts more than $500,000 (or $1 million for construction of a public facility) large contractors and subcontractors must submit subcontracting plans containing specific percentage goals for small businesses, HUBZone small businesses, small disadvantaged businesses, and women-owned small businesses.

"subcontracting plans contain a description of the methods and efforts used to assure that small business enterprises have an equitable opportunity to compete for subcontracts.

"subcontracting plans be submitted by contractors for review prior to the award of any contract; failure to comply in good faith with its approved plan may subject the contractor to liquidated damages or termination for default."[1]

billion with minority-owned businesses in 2004 and an additional $600 million with women-owned businesses. Spending with WBE and MBEs accounted for 8.1 percent of Ford's total procurement budget in 2004.

Ford has aggressively leveraged its position as a diversity leader to extract similar commitments from its largest suppliers. Ford's second-tier sourcing program requires its major contractors to develop their own supplier-diversity programs. As a result, Ford's 550 largest suppliers reported economic activity of $12 billion with suppliers owned by women, people of color, and people with disabilities, $1.8 billion of which was spent directly because of Ford.

Ford prime supplier Johnson Controls Inc. (JCI) purchased more than $1 billion from minority- and women-owned businesses in 2003 and was named to the Billion Dollar Roundtable, joining Ford as one of only 12 U.S. companies to have reached that spending level at that time.

In addition, companies in other industries are realizing the benefits. Wal-Mart (No. 29 on The 2005 DiversityInc Top 50 Companies for Diversity list) is one example of a company that recognized that its supplier-diversity program needed some work. The company's diversity department, launched in November 2003, has worked to increase the retailer's percentage of MBE and WBE suppliers by 23 percent. That's still only 2 percent of the company's total procurement budget, but it's progress.[5]

Because it may be difficult for small businesses to satisfy the demands of serving Wal-Mart on a national scale, the diversity department is exploring areas where small suppliers can partner with individual stores. One example is Anaheim, Calif.–based LuLu's Dessert, owned by Maria de Lourdes "LuLu" Sobrino. The company produces ready-to-eat gelatins, which Wal-Mart has sold since 2001 and now carries in more than 1,000 of its 5,200 stores.[6] The company is working to carry the product outside of the United States and added LuLu's Desserts to its Sam's Clubs in Mexico.[7]

THE DIVERSITYINC TOP 10 COMPANIES FOR SUPPLIER DIVERSITY

When compiling the DiversityInc Top 10 Companies for Supplier Diversity list, a number of criteria were considered. DiversityInc looked at the percentage of the company's procurement budget spent with first-

and second-tier minority- and women-owned businesses. In addition, companies were asked whether second-tier supplier diversity was mandated, whether WBE and MBE suppliers received third-party certification, and whether the corporation included all small businesses when counting "diverse" suppliers. Companies also were asked whether they help their diverse suppliers through educational programs, loans and community support.[8]

Average Dollar Amounts With Diverse Suppliers

Tier I	
Top 10 for Supplier Diversity	More than $1 Billion
Rest of Top 50	Up to $500,000
Companies 91+	Up to $100,000

Tier II	
Top 10 for Supplier Diversity	$500,000
Rest of Top 50	Up to $100,000
Companies 91+	Up to $10,000

Source: DiversityInc

GOVERNMENT PROGRAMS

The SBA has set up programs to help MBEs, WBEs and disadvantaged businesses.

HUBZone Empowerment Contracting Program: "The HUBZone Empowerment Contracting Program stimulates economic development and creates jobs in urban and rural communities by providing federal contracting preferences to small businesses. These preferences go to small businesses that obtain HUBZone (Historically Underutilized Business Zone) certification in part by employing staff members who live in a HUBZone. The company also must maintain a principal office in one of these specially designated areas. The program resulted from provisions contained in the Small Business Reauthorization Act of 1997."[9]

8(a) Program: The SBA's 8(a) BD Program, named for a section of the Small Business Act, is a business-development program created to help small, disadvantaged businesses compete in the U.S. economy and access the federal procurement market. An application must be filed and the applicant firm must meet certain criteria, including being a small business that is unconditionally owned and controlled by one or more socially and economically disadvantaged individuals who are of good character and citizens of the United States, and must demonstrate potential for success.[10]

THIRD-PARTY CERTIFICATION

Third-party certification through a reputable organization can be an important tool for small businesses, and it gives your company the assurance that your suppliers are comprised of the ownership they claim. All of the DiversityInc Top 10 Companies for Supplier Diversity have certification requirements for their small-business suppliers versus an average of 93 percent of the rest of the Top 50 and 65 percent of companies ranked higher than 91.

To be eligible for government set-asides or support, small companies look to the SBA as the source of certification for diverse businesses. Requirements among states and municipalities also vary. However, different corporations will have varying requirements for certification as well, and here, there are additional sources of third-party certification.

In the private sector, the NMSDC is the main certifying organization for MBEs. The Women Business Enterprise National Council (WBENC) and the National Women Business Owners Corporation (NWBOC) are the main certifying organizations for WBEs. There are no certifying organizations for disabled veterans or other small or disadvantaged business enterprises, other than the SBA.

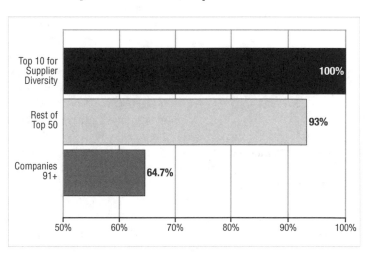

Third-Party Certification Required

- Top 10 for Supplier Diversity: **100%**
- Rest of Top 50: **93%**
- Companies 91+: **64.7%**

Source: DiversityInc
Top 10 Companies for Supplier Diversity
Companies Ranked 91 and Higher on the Top 50 Survey

Most certifying organizations generally require that a business be at least 51 percent owned, managed and operated by an individual or individuals who reflect the indication on the certification. For instance, a WBE would be at least 51 percent owned, managed and operated by one or more women. Here are the major public and private-sector agencies and their requirements:

Small Business Administration (SBA): As they are defined by legislation, government certification standards are complex and detailed. The SBA currently uses the North American Industrial Classification System (NAICS) to define "small business," which, as of October 2000, replaced the Standard Industrial Classification (SIC) Codes.[11]

National Minority Supplier Development Council (NMSDC): According to the NMSDC, "A minority-owned business is a for-profit enterprise, regardless of size, physically located in the United States or its trust territories, which is owned, operated and controlled by minority group members. 'Minority group members' are United States citizens who are Asian, Black, Hispanic and Native American. Ownership by minority individuals means the business is at least 51 percent owned by such individuals or, in the case of a publicly-owned business, at least 51 percent of the stock is owned by one or more such individuals. Further, the management and daily operations are controlled by those minority group members."[12]

Understanding the Certifications

Launching a successful supplier-diversity program means understanding the terminology.

Minority Business Enterprises (MBEs): This description is applied to a business that is at least 51 percent owned, managed and controlled by one or more individuals, male or female, who are black, Latino, Native American or Asian American.

Women-Owned Business Enterprises (WBEs): Businesses that are at least 51 percent owned, managed and controlled by a woman are eligible for this certification.

Disabled Veteran–Owned Businesses: Businesses that are at least 51 percent owned, managed and controlled by an individual or individuals who have physical or mental impairments that substantially limit one or more of such persons in major life activities often are called disabled-owned businesses. When that disability was sustained during active service in one of the U.S. armed forces, the business is called a "disabled-veteran business enterprise," or DVBE, or "service-disabled veteran" (SDV) business enterprise.

Disadvantaged Business Enterprise (DBE): Each of these companies also can be called a "Small Disadvantaged Business" (SBD), which combines the definition of a DBE with the Small Business Administration (SBA)'s definition of a small business.

The SBD certification ensures that small businesses that are owned and controlled by socially and economically disadvantaged individuals meeting certain specific criteria are eligible for certain benefits, including: "Under the government's reformed affirmative action rules, small disadvantaged businesses are eligible for price evaluation adjustments of up to 10 percent when bidding on federal contracts in certain industries."[3]

Several other acronym variations exist, such as MWBE for minority- and women-owned business enterprises and DVMWBE for disabled veteran, minority and women business enterprises, and may crop up in discussions of supplier diversity.

The NMSDC also offers a series of definitions of which demographic segments it considers minorities. The organization also offers Tier II certification for Minority Controlled Organizations. According to the organization, "A minority business may be certified as a minority 'controlled' enterprise if the minority owners own at least 30 percent of the economic equity of the firm. This occurs when non-minority institutional investors contribute a majority of the firm's risk capital (equity). Under this special circumstance, a business may be certified as a minority 'controlled' firm if the following criteria are met: A) Minority management/owners control the day-to-day operations of the firm; B) Minority management/owners retain a majority (no less than 51 percent) of the firm's 'voting equity'; and C) Minority owners operationally control the board of directors (i.e., must appoint a majority of the board of directors)."

Growth Of Minority-Owned Businesses, 1992–1997
Percent change, number of businesses

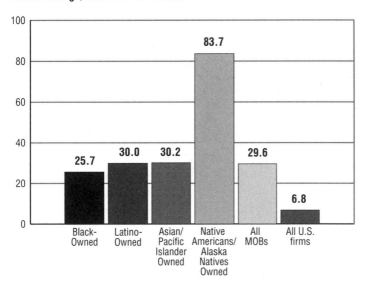

National Women Business Owners Corporation Network (NWBOC):

"There are two basic principles of business, ownership and control, which must apply to your business in order to be eligible for certification by NWBOC. Ownership: A woman or women own(s) one of the following: 100 percent of the assets of a sole proprietorship; at least 51 percent of the equity interests in a partnership; or at least 51 percent of each of the classes of outstanding equity securities in a corporation; or at least 51 percent of the membership interests in a limited-liability company. Control: A woman or women control(s) one of the following: 100 percent of the control of a sole proprietorship; or at least 51 percent of the control of a general partnership; woman owner is the general partner and, if there is more than one general partner, the managing general partner, of a limited partnership or limited liability partnership; or, the woman owner is entitled to appoint a majority of a corporate board of directors. A woman or women is/are the sole manager, able to appoint unconditionally the majority of managers of a manager-managed LLC or has 51 percent control of a member-managed LLC."[13]

Women's Business Enterprise National Council (WBENC): "Fifty-one percent ownership by a woman or women … Proof of effective management of the business (operating position, by-laws, hire-fire and other decision-making role) … Control of the business as evidenced by signature role on loans, leases and contracts … U.S. Citizenship or Resident Alien Status."[14]

Women are not considered a minority by the federal government. Women interested in contracting with the government simply have to say that they own the majority of their businesses as well as control their companies' management and daily business operations. Companies that find the most value in certification are those that wish to become suppliers to large corporations.

Second-Tier Diversity: Questions You Need to Ask Your Suppliers

To effectively track your diversity spending, you need to know about the diversity spending of your suppliers. Here are some of the questions you should be asking:

- Do you currently subcontract work to third-party vendors?
- If so, what measures do you take to ensure that your procurement practices are inclusive?
- What dollar amount do you spend with WBEs, MBEs, SDVs and disadvantaged businesses?
- What percentage is that of your total procurement budget?
- How will you report such spending to our company?
- Do you track which of your suppliers use subcontractors?
- If so, do you require or request that they use inclusive practices when hiring suppliers?
- Do you require them to report their spending with diverse businesses?
- How will you report to us their spending with WBEs, MBEs, SDVs and disadvantaged businesses?

The reverse is true for companies owned by disabled veterans or people with disabilities. The government will require that they meet certain criteria, but there is no national standard in the public sector. In addition, standards for what constitutes a disabled-owned or SDV business vary from company to company. However, some companies require that businesses owned by disabled veteran entrepreneurs register with the Service Disabled Veterans Group, Inc. (SDVG), which is a for-profit corporation owned by a memorial trust, benefiting military veterans who were killed in action, prisoners of war or missing in action, or those deceased from service-incurred disability. The company teams SDVs and other operations with larger corporation entities known as Patriot Partners.[15]

BREAKING DOWN THE SUPPLY-SIDE DEMOGRAPHICS

Finding diverse suppliers is becoming easier as their numbers swell. Mirroring demographic shifts in the population, minority-owned businesses (MBEs) are growing faster than the national average. While the number of U.S. businesses grew by 10 percent between 1997 and 2002, the growth rate for minority- and women-owned businesses ranged from 67 percent for native Hawaiian and Pacific Islander-owned businesses to 20 percent for businesses owned by women, according to preliminary estimates released in 2005 by the Census Bureau.[16]

Minority- and women-owned businesses also experienced higher revenue growth than businesses owned by whites. Black-owned firms had the highest growth, at 30 percent, versus 5 percent for white-owned firms and a national average for all firms of 22 percent.[17]

Women-owned businesses (WBE) in the United States increased 20 percent to 6.5 million, twice as fast as all businesses between 1997 and 2002, excluding publicly held corporations. Women-owned businesses generated 950.6 billion in receipts in 2002, up 16 percent from 1997.[18]

Expansion rates among businesses owned by Latinos, Asian Americans and Native Americans also were larger than businesses owned by whites. While black-owned businesses expanded at a slightly lower rate than those owned by whites, Latino- and black-owned employer establishments had the lowest contraction rates.[19]

TRACKING SPENDING

All supplier spending is not created equal. There is an important difference between supplier-diversity spending and share of spending, which looks at dollars spent with diverse suppliers spent among all suppliers. In 2003, members of the NMSDC Network, which certifies and matches qualified minority-owned businesses including 3,500 corporate members in 39 regional councils across the country, spent an estimated $80.2 billion with businesses owned by Asian Americans, blacks, Latinos and Native Americans.[20]

Still, companies need to look at more than the raw numbers of how much they're spending with diverse suppliers and also compare those figures to the bigger picture of their overall procurement budgets. A company may spend more than a billion dollars with diverse suppliers. However, if that number represents a single-digit percentage of the total spending budget, suddenly the large number isn't as impressive.

It's important to be clear about how your company is reporting its supplier spending as well. Since there are no universally accepted standards for calculating the amount spent on diverse suppliers, reporting may vary greatly from company to company. Many companies include businesses owned by people of color or women, service-disabled veterans, HUBZone businesses or the amorphous category "small business" in their reporting.[21]

SUBCONTRACTORS AND SECOND-TIER SPENDING

Supplier-diversity programs must not only take into account direct spending with suppliers, called first-tier suppliers, but also with those companies' providers and subcontractors, referred to as "second-tier" spending. All of the 2005 DiversityInc Top 10 Companies for Supplier Diversity require their suppliers to report second-tier spending. That's 25 percent more than the average of those companies on The 2005 DiversityInc Top 50 Companies for Diversity list and 60 percent more than the average of companies ranked higher than 91 on the list.[22]

To explain the concept more clearly, consider the following analogy:

The Department of Defense hires Lockheed Martin as a first-tier supplier to manufacture 85 airplanes. At a hypothetical $1 million per plane, Lockheed will receive gross revenue of $85 million for the project. However, since Lockheed doesn't have all of the parts and labor to make the planes from scratch, it must hire suppliers of various products and services, or "subcontractors," to fulfill its obligation to the DOD.

Thanks to legislation, such as Public Law 95-507, Lockheed had to guarantee that at least 5 percent of spending on subcontractors would be done with diverse suppliers. As a result, Lockheed has hired Joe's Wing Company to handle a portion of the plane manufacturing. Joe, who is black, and his company are the second tier in the chain.

Minority Business Ownership Compared With Minority Population, 1982–2002
By percent change

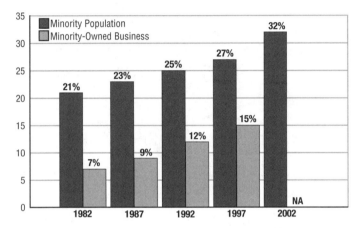

Source: Small Business Administration, "Dynamics of Minority-Owned Employer Establishments"

Recognizing that many MBEs, WBEs or disadvantaged businesses aren't large enough to handle the corporate equivalent of an $85-million contract, large companies and the NMSDC have developed second-tier spending goals to ensure that diverse suppliers get a piece of the pie. This has not been without controversy since, unlike in the public sector, private companies cannot be compelled to spend a set amount with diverse suppliers.

A significant issue is how companies report their second-tier spending. Companies that roll first- and second-tier figures into one number may give an inaccurate picture of their spending. The standard practice is to report the spending separately. At the very least, if companies combine the two figures, they should make this clear in their reporting.

BILLION DOLLAR ROUNDTABLE
The Billion Dollar Roundtable (BDR) was founded in 2001 by two diversity directors and the publisher of a regional business publication.

It was founded to provide a top-level forum for BDR members to share strategies and ideas and to leverage the combined knowledge of BDR members for use by others.

Procter & Gamble (P&G), No. 27 on The 2005 DiversityInc Top 50 Companies for Diversity list, and Toyota Motor North America are the newest additions to the BDR, an initiative honoring companies that spend more than $1 billion annually with minority- and women-owned businesses. The latest inductees join 12 other companies that collectively devoted more than $24 billion on supply-chain-diversity spend in 2004.[23]

The dozen other companies with seats at the BDR:
Altria Group (No. 1 on The 2005 DiversityInc Top 50 Companies for Diversity list and No. 6 on the 2005 Top 10 Companies for Supplier Diversity)
AT&T Corp.
DaimlerChrysler Corp. (one of DiversityInc's 25 Noteworthy Companies in 2005 and No. 3 on the 2005 Top 10 Companies for Supplier Diversity)
Ford Motor Co. (No. 11 on The 2005 DiversityInc Top 50 Companies for Diversity list and No. 2 on the 2005 Top 10 Companies for Supplier Diversity)
General Motors Co. (No. 48 on The 2005 DiversityInc Top 50 Companies for Diversity list and No. 5 on the 2005 Top 10 Companies for Supplier Diversity)
IBM
Johnson Controls
Lockheed Martin Corp.
Lucent Technologies
SBC Communications (No. 15 on The 2005 DiversityInc Top 50 Companies for Diversity list)
Verizon Communications (No. 9 on The 2005 DiversityInc Top 50 Companies for Diversity list)
Wal-Mart Stores (No. 29 on The 2005 DiversityInc Top 50 Companies for Diversity list)

LAYING THE FOUNDATION FOR SUCCESS

How do companies lay a foundation for supplier-diversity success? Like other diversity initiatives, it starts with a comprehensive approach to making it work.

At some companies, every purchase—from garbage-can liners to legal services—is evaluated against supplier-diversity goals. Supplier-diversity experts are accorded budgets and respect; measurement tools track progress and pitfalls. There's a broad understanding of demographics: Minority-owned businesses represent one of the nation's fastest-growing business segments and have assumed an increasingly important role in economic growth. The nation's largest companies are expected to spend $70 billion—4 percent of their combined procurement budgets—with companies owned by women and people of color.[24]

Of course, each of those companies started from scratch, building quality supplier-diversity programs one critical step at a time. Here is their basic blueprint:[25]

Define the Business Case: Companies that sell their goods directly to consumers have been particularly astute at drawing a link between supplier diversity and solid sales. Strong suppliers provide jobs and paychecks, strengthening communities, increasing affluence and creating potential new customers. With new vibrant emerging markets among people of color and other population segments, demographic data, both external and internal, helps to build the business case.[26]

Examine the Existing Supplier Base: Supplier-diversity directors are sometimes surprised to learn they already have contracts with women and minority businesses. Existing relationships with successful and respected suppliers can form the foundation of a formal supplier-diversity program.[27]

Set Clear Goals: Identifying existing suppliers often helps the company set the supplier-diversity bar higher than it might otherwise be inclined. But even if diverse suppliers are absent altogether, a company needs to establish a realistic spending goal that takes into account total procurement spending and the dollar value of existing long-term contracts. The goal can be revised as contracts end.[28]

Engage the CEO: Supplier-diversity programs can survive without a true commitment from the top, but they cannot thrive. A strong program requires the dedication of personnel and budget, as well as the understanding that it will take years, not months, to build a quality supplier-diversity operation.[29]

Court Middle Managers: CEO commitment gets a program off the ground, but it takes the cooperation of purchasing managers and buyers to keep it up and running. Encourage middle managers to share their concerns and their ideas. Recognize that they may have longstanding supplier relationships in place and contracts that cannot be cancelled overnight.[30]

Develop a Corporate-Commitment Statement: A statement of principles and practices can help the company communicate goals and objectives. The statement also should offer a clear indication of the company's purpose in creating a supplier-diversity program and the company's expectations.[31]

Provide Loans to Diverse Suppliers

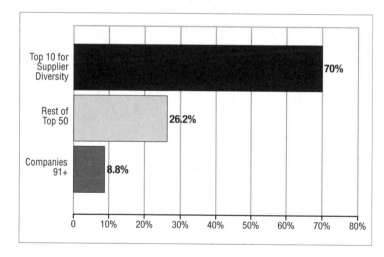

Source: DiversityInc
Top 10 Companies for Supplier Diversity
Companies Ranked 91 and Higher on the Top 50 Survey

Recruit for Passion: Successful supplier-diversity directors are passionate about their work. It's not a job for someone looking for a peaceful corporate backwater. As their programs grow, directors often are on the road. The best directors invest a lot of time in bringing together buyers and business owners—a job that can't always be done between 9 a.m. and 5 p.m.[32]

Benchmark: WBENC and the NMSDC are best known for certifying companies as women- or minority-owned, but they also serve gathering point for supplier-diversity executives. Both organizations, along with industry trade councils and chambers of commerce, offer a range of formal meetings that allow supplier-diversity program managers to compare notes with their peers in a specific industry or geographic area. These meetings also give supplier-diversity directors an opportunity to network with others, which can be a good opportunity to share ideas with others who are implementing their own supplier-diversity programs.[33]

Location within the reporting structure is also important for the success of a supplier-diversity department, which should be located within a company's procurement sector. At the Top 10 Companies for Supplier Diversity, 90 percent of supplier-diversity heads report to head of procurement versus 66 percent of rest of the Top 50 and 60 percent of companies rated 90 and higher.

[1] U.S. Small Business Administration, "Subcontracting Opportunities," http://www.sba.gov/businessop/basics/subcontracting.html

[2] *DiversityInc*, "Top 50 Companies for Diversity, Top 10 Companies for Supplier Diversity," June 2005, page 76

[3] U.S. Small Business Administration, "About Small Disadvantaged Business Certification," http://www.sba.gov/sdb/indexaboutsdb.html

[4] *DiversityInc*, "M-Tier: The Next Generation of Supplier Development," by Peter Ortiz, March 2005, page 70

[5] *DiversityInc*, "The Big Shocker: How Did Wal-Mart Get on the Top 50 List?" June 2005, page 124

[6] Ibid, page 127

[7] Ibid

[8] *DiversityInc*, "Top 50 Companies for Diversity, Top 10 Companies for Supplier Diversity," June 2005, page 76

[9] Information on the HubZone program is available online at http://www.sba.gov/hubzone/

[10] Information on the 8(a) Program is available online at http://www.sba.gov/8abd/indexfaqs.html

[11] Information on NAICS standards is available online at www.sba.gov/size and http://www.wrf.com/publication.cfm?publication_id=11539

[12] Information about NMSDC certification is available online at http://www.nmsdcus.org/who_we_are/certification.html

[13] Information about NWBOC certification is available online at http://www.nwboc.org/certapp.html

[14] Information about WBENC certification is available online at http://www.wbenc.org/certification/index.html

[15] Information on SDV certification is available online at: http://www.asdv.org/BUSRES/index.cfm

[16] U.S. Census Bureau, "2002 Survey of Business Owners Preliminary Estimates of Business Ownership by Gender, Hispanic or Latino Origin, and Race: 2002," http:www.census.gov/csd/sbo/sector/sec00.HTM

[17] Ibid

[18] Ibid

[19] U.S. Small Business Administration, "Dynamics of Minority-Owned Employer Establishments, 1997-2001," February 2005, page 5. http://www.sba.gov/advo/research/rs251tot.pdf

[20] NMSDC Web site: http://www.nmsdcus.org/who_we_are/procurement.html and http://www.nmsdcus.org/who_we_are/purpose.html

[21] *DiversityInc*, "Are Your Supplier-Diversity Numbers Inflated?" by Yoji Cole, October/November 2003, page 97

[22] *DiversityInc*, "Top 50 Companies for Diversity, Top 10 Companies for Supplier Diversity," June 2005, page 76

[23] DiversityInc.com, "P&G, Toyota Get Seats at Billion-Dollar Round-table," by DiversityInc staff, May 20, 2005

[24] *DiversityInc*, "From the Ground Up: how to Lay a Foundation for Supplier-Diversity Success," by Linda Bean, April/May 2004

[25] Ibid

[26] Ibid

[27] Ibid

[28] Ibid

[29] Ibid

[30] Ibid

[31] Ibid

[32] Ibid

[33] Ibid

M ore companies are adopting strong diversity initiatives, recognizing them as essential investments. Companies that aren't taking diversity seriously need to examine what a lack of inclusiveness is costing them. Instead of trying to cut costs related to recruitment, training and other human-capital issues (for more on costs, see Chapter 8), companies should be looking at the true cost of not maintaining a diverse work force.

As the nation continues to shift dramatically, so have the centers of buying power. Companies that are not poised to take advantage of these fundamental changes in the marketplace will lose their competitive edge.

Buying Power of Emerging and Untapped Markets

The nation's buying power, the total after-tax personal income available for spending on goods and services, will increase by 159 percent between 1990 and 2009.[1] Overall buying-power growth has been somewhat uneven in recent years and includes a mild recession in the first two years of the span, and another in 2001. Gross domestic product is expected to increase moderately through 2009.[2] States with low costs of doing business, affordable housing, communications and transportation infrastructure, and favorable regulatory environments are fueling the growth, attracting domestic and international businesses.[3]

CHAPTER 6

The Cost of Being Homogenous

As covered in Chapter 1, there are a number of important economic shifts taking place among various population segments, including people of color, individuals with disabilities, GLBTs and women. Each of these segments has a significant and growing amount of discretionary income. Smart companies are taking a close look at how to better serve the needs of each population group as well as how to best communicate the company's offerings to them. Having a diverse employee base facilitates this analysis.

Missed Opportunities
and Customer Affinity

In order to identify and capitalize on these emerging and untapped markets, companies need employees who understand them. Accepting stereotypes or myths can be costly and lead to missed opportunities or, worse, offending consumers.

PepsiCo has found that fostering a greater understanding of customers is adding to its bottom line. Studying ethnic markets led to new prod-

Multicultural Missteps Can Be Costly

Multicultural missteps were beginning to define Abercrombie & Fitch in communities of color and ended up costing the New Albany, Ohio–based retailer more than offended customers. Following a three-year Equal Employment Opportunity Commission (EEOC) investigation and a class-action employment-discrimination lawsuit filed in 2003, the company agreed to a $50-million settlement and signed a consent decree that requires it to implement several diversity initiatives within six years.

Of the $50 million, $10 million was earmarked for attorneys' fees, the diversity initiatives and monitoring the company's progress. The remaining $40 million was to be shared among the 17 named and other potential plaintiffs who were expected to reap between $5,000 and $39,000 each, depending on the number of class-action plaintiffs who came forward to collect. The company hired a diversity director.

In April of 2005, Abercrombie & Fitch announced it would give a $300,000 grant to the United Negro College Fund (UNCF) to establish the UNCF/Abercrombie & Fitch Scholarship Program. In an interview with *DiversityInc* magazine, Todd Corley, Abercrombie's first vice president of diversity, said the company would take steps toward improving its relationship with people of color. "It's huge—they are our customers," he said. "They have to know we're committed. That's critical to our success."

In addition to hiring practices that plaintiffs say relegated people of color to stock rooms and late-night shifts, in 2002 Abercrombie & Fitch angered the Asian-American community with T-shirts, including one that featured stereotypical caricatures. One featured a cartoon image of two Asians wearing rice-paddy hats with a slogan between them that read "Wong Brothers Laundry Service: Two Wongs Can Make It White."

Abercrombie & Fitch stores had not traditionally been very welcoming for shoppers of color. Store walls rarely featured models of color; few even feature brunettes. The company's Web site received an F grade from DiversityInc's "Scorecard" because of lack of faces of color and information on diversity management and inclusive-hiring practices.

Since then, Abercrombie has added diversity information, including career opportunities for people of color, to its homepage and has launched several external diversity initiatives, including a partnership with INROADS, a nonprofit organization that helps establish internships for people of color, to increase the number of people of color in the retail industry.[5]

ucts such as guacamole-flavored Doritos chips and Gatorade Xtremo, targeted toward Latinos, and Mountain Dew Code Red, which appeals to blacks. These additions to Pepsi's offerings added an estimated one percentage point of the company's 2003 revenue growth of 7.4 percent, or about $250 million.[4]

Obsolescence and Customer Alienation

Being inclusive puts a corporate finger on the pulse of emerging ethnic, gender and lifestyle markets. Misunderstanding these markets can lead to alienation, while missteps in communication or adopting stereotypes as fact can cause companies to falter in acquiring new business. When a company reflects its marketplace in its work force, it is better able to understand the needs of its market as they evolve.

Conversely, companies out of step with the changing marketplace risk going the way of the typewriter manufacturer. If that seems unlikely, consider this: 50 percent of the 1980 Fortune 500 are out of business today.

Reduced Employee Retention

In addition to identifying external markets, a failure to diversify can create internal problems. With the great care and expense that companies devote to recruiting and training the best employees, retention of those human assets is always a corporate priority. When companies fail to retain valuable employees, they spend more in recruiting and training new employees.

> When companies fail to retain valuable employees, they spend more in recruiting and training new employees.

Negative Public Perception

When companies fail to be inclusive, public perception can be negatively affected. Publicity surrounding multicultural missteps, racism, ageism, sexism or other policies that discriminate against a segment of the population can lead to customer alienation or even organized boycotts. High-profile criticism of a company can even cause share prices to decrease or can destroy

> Publicity surrounding multicultural missteps, racism, ageism, sexism or other policies that discriminate against a segment of the population can lead to customer alienation or even organized boycotts.

How Wal-Mart Made The 2005 DiversityInc Top 50 Companies for Diversity List

Mired in diversity-related trouble, Wal-Mart was fighting the nation's largest diversity-related lawsuit, had hired undocumented workers and forced mom-and-pop businesses to close. It had little supplier diversity and was routinely skewered for its lack of diversity by *DiversityInc*, which ran headlines like "Wal-Mart Diversity Head Can't Back Claims with Numbers."[7]

Yet the company ranked No. 29 on The DiversityInc Top 50 Companies for Diversity list in 2005. After instituting a diversity department in 2003, the company went to work overhauling its diversity efforts. Prior to that, the company had only had a cadre of loose diversity initiatives. Now located in Bentonville, Ark., Wal-Mart began focusing its managers and officers on recruiting women, people of color, GLBTs and people with disabilities, as well as on retaining and marketing to the consumers they represent.[8]

Wal-Mart's board of directors made diversity-goal achievement a performance measure for officers and managers. If an officer did not meet his or her diversity goals, he or she lost 7.5 percent of his or her bonus. In contrast, most companies in the Top 50 give managers extra money if they meet their goals.[9]

To measure recruitment efforts, officers are required to hire the percentage of qualified people from a designated group who apply. For example, if 40 percent of the people who apply for a position are female, then the hiring officer is expected to place 40 percent women. Officers and managers also are required to attend external diversity events, part of their "good-faith effort goals," which can include participating in leadership events, such as the company's "Women in Leadership" and "Minorities in Leadership" semi-nars. Wal-Mart also requires its managers to mentor at least three people who are of a different gender, race or background.[10]

As a result, new hires are 37 percent people of color and 54 percent women, while management consists of 21 percent people of color, according to data for 2004. Of the company's top 10 percent highest-paid employees, 45 percent are women and 21 percent are people of color. On its board of directors, 29 percent are people of color and 15 percent are women.[11]

Every officer, including the company CEO, went through diversity training at the home office in Bentonville. This year, all members of management and hourly supervisors within 90 days of either their hire date or the date they were promoted into their current position must go through diversity training.[12]

To better serve the communities in which it does business, Wal-Mart has begun to tailor its product mix on a regional basis. For example, a Wal-Mart in a heavily Latino area will feature foods and spices special to Latinos, while another location in a heavily Asian-American area will feature items special to them. The company also has launched affinity groups to gain further insights into its consumer base and has launched significant supplier-diversity initiatives.[13]

Of course, the company still has a way to go before it overcomes years of diversity neglect. Wal-Mart still faces a massive class-action gender-discrimination lawsuit, and its supplier diversity numbers aren't at enviable levels yet. However, the progress thus far has earned it a coveted spot on The DiversityInc Top 50 Companies for Diversity list, and company officials say they strive for better showings on the list in future.[14]

relationships with valued employees and suppliers who may feel betrayed by negative policies, comments or other signs of a culture that does not value diversity.

When taped remarks of Texaco employees making racial epithets were made public by plaintiffs' attorneys in a class-action discrimination lawsuit in 1996, Texaco officials acted almost immediately to quell the furor that erupted. Texaco Chairman Peter Bijur, confronted with a boycott threat from the black community as well as an onslaught of negative publicity, apologized to the company's black employees for the comments and behavior of the company's executives and ordered a settlement of the discrimination litigation. Eleven days after the remarks were made public, the company settled the lawsuit for $176.1 million.[6]

Litigation

In addition to the costs of missed opportunities, obsolescence and employee turnover, companies that resist inclusive policies may find themselves with another set of hefty costs: attorney fees and fines. In 2004, the EEOC received slightly fewer complaints. Even though complaints have fallen, however, 40 lawsuits filed with the EEOC in 2004 cost corporations $74.3 million.

Companies that find themselves looking at employees who all appear the same are not only missing key opportunities, but they may find themselves on the receiving end of charges of discrimination—yet another reason to keep the company work force diverse.

[1] Selig Center Report, page 2

[2] Ibid

[3] Ibid

[4] *The Wall Street Journal*, "Pepsi, Vowing Diversity Isn't Just Image Polish, Seeks Inclusive Culture" by Chad Terhune, April 19, 2005

[5] Abercrombie & Fitch Web site, http://www.abercrombie.com/anf/lifestyles/html/homepage.html (Click on Diversity & Inclusion link)

[6] DiversityInc.com, "Lott's Two Big Mistakes – Ignoring Black Republicans & Not Acting Quickly," by Linda Bean, December 18, 2002

[7] *DiversityInc*, "The Big Shocker: How did Wal-Mart Get on the Top 50 List?" June 2005, page 124

[8] Ibid

[9] Ibid, page 126

[10] Ibid

[11] Ibid

[12] Ibid

[13] Ibid

[14] Ibid

D iversity leaders in corporations must provide a means of measurement that quantifies return on investment and proves to upper management that diversity produces bottom-line benefits, including bringing in new revenue streams. Simply measuring the number of people of color in an organization isn't enough. Equal Employment Opportunity or affirmative-action numbers tell a limited portion of the story.

Metrics should be applied to all business units and must be reported directly to the CEO and top management. As we've seen in previous chapters, diversity programs work best when compensation, especially for senior management, is tied to these metrics.

MEASURING YOUR COMPANY'S DIVERSITY

While the most common tools for measuring diversity usually are personnel-related, including breaking down the demographics of the employee base, companies in The DiversityInc Top 50 Companies for Diversity must provide data in four separate areas:

- Human capital
- CEO commitment
- Supplier diversity
- Corporate communications (internal and external)

CHAPTER 7

How Does Your Organization Measure Up?

The most common, and usually the easiest, diversity measurement is that of diversity of personnel and management. While some companies may use Equal Employment Opportunity and affirmative-action numbers, these numbers tell only a partial story. Companies need to measure more detailed demographics beyond just race/ethnicity and gender. Ensuring that the culture is inclusive of GLBTs, who may not readily self-identify; people with disabilities, who may not self-identify and whose disabilities may not be immediately evident; and aging workers, who may be reluctant to share their ages, takes more than just guessing where an employee fits within such broad categories.

In addition, diversity metrics need to evaluate an organization's culture and how well it is doing in creating an environment where diversity truly is valued. Metrics also need to be applied to marketplace issues—both the changing population demographics discussed in Chapter 1 and the portion of that market that the company is capturing with its sales and marketing efforts. Companies should be tracking how their diversity efforts impact such issues as retention. This saves the company money, as well as outreach, which can create new revenue streams.

> Companies should be tracking how their diversity efforts impact such issues as retention. This saves the company money, as well as outreach, which can create new revenue streams.

MEASURING THE PEOPLE

To get a more accurate measurement of internal diversity among employees, companies can encourage their employees to share their backgrounds, abilities and orientations by offering incentives to do so. For instance, domestic-partner benefits can be a strong motivating factor for a GLBT individual to share his or her sexual orientation with an employer.

Companies should work to capture aggregate data about the numbers of people of color, women, people with disabilities, GLBTs and aging workers that they have within their ranks, and at every level. It's not enough to do a simple head count. Instead, companies must analyze their current employee base to find out:

Does diversity exist at every level of the company?

It's not enough to have a certain number of diverse employees—they need to be woven throughout the fabric of the company's work force and they particularly need to be in management ranks and in the pipeline for senior decision-making positions. Examine what percentage of middle and senior managers are women, black, Latino, Asian American, Native American, GLBTs and people with disabilities. How do those numbers compare with the general breakdown of the work force? Similarly, among the highest-paid employees, how many are people of color, women, GLBTs or people with disabilities?

Is the company working to recruit more diverse workers into its talent pipeline?

The number of new hires over the past year may tell one story, but the breakdown of those new hires may reveal a clearer picture. Were new hires over the past year inclusive of black, Latino, Asian-American, Native American, GLBT, or older workers or workers with disabilities? Did the company take measures to recruit employees from these groups? With myriad options available for recruitment of a diverse employee base, including Web sites, newspaper classified ads, job fairs, on-campus recruitment,

Were new hires over the past year inclusive of black, Latino, Asian-American, Native American, GLBT, or older workers or workers with disabilities?

working with professional organizations and the like, companies should be aggressively pursuing a variety of recruitment methods for diverse employees.

Who's being hired?

How does the breakdown of new hires fall across various levels of staff and management? If employees of color, employees with disabilities, GLBT employees, women employees and older workers aren't being hired for management and growth-track positions with regularity, it's time to look at why.

Who's being promoted?

Just as a company looks at who's being hired and where they work, it's also critical to look at the numbers of employees who are advancing within the organization. Are appropriate numbers of blacks, Latinos, Asian Americans, Native Americans, women, people with disabilities, older workers and GLBTs moving up the ranks? From those individuals who are being promoted, the company should be working to harvest information, such as in which employee-development programs the individual participated; if the individual has a mentor within the company; and which organizational resources the promoted employee believes are most valuable to his or her career development.

Who's staying—and who's leaving?

Retention rate is defined by DiversityInc as the reverse of turnover rate minus involuntary terminations, such as firing or layoffs. Within your company, which workers are being retained? If the company is losing a greater percentage of people of color, men, women, GLBTs, people with disabilities or aging workers, it's a good idea to look at why this talent is leaving the company. Is it a failure of the culture to be inclusive? Or are there other factors that make the workplace less attractive to these groups? The answers could lead to measures that result in great savings of talent—and money—through increased retention.

Clearly, the number of employees of different races/ethnicities, genders, sexual orientations, levels of disability and ages tells only part of the story. Companies that are truly committed to diversity work ensure that their inclusive culture permeates their organizations from the boardrooms to the mailrooms.

HUMAN-CAPITAL-MEASUREMENT TOOLS

How can you capture all of this information? There are a number of tools that companies can use to examine the various facets of their human capital and to determine whether their efforts to create inclusive cultures are working. These include:

■ **Employee-attitude surveys:** Organizations should survey employees on a regular basis to determine how they feel about the company and its diversity initiatives. Such surveys may capture more honest feedback if they are anonymous, but even if they are not, employees should feel free to give an honest evaluation of their feelings about the company's level of diversity and success at creating a culture of inclusion.

■ **Focus groups:** Gathering small groups of employees for feedback sessions, and to gather their perceptions about such topics as recruitment of diverse employees, training, mentoring programs and other methods of fostering cultural competence, can result in firsthand discussion and feedback of these important topics. Focus-group participants should be encouraged to be honest in their comments, without fear of reprisal, and focus groups should also be led by a skilled and objective focus-group moderator.

■ **Internal audits:** Organizations should regularly review employee data to determine how the numbers are shaping up. Reviewing data on salary and promotion levels, percentage of diverse managers, retention rates and other employee facts and figures can give companies a snapshot of how their diversity efforts are working.

■ **Training and education evaluations:** Training evaluations can provide insight into how receptive an organization's employees are to diversity initiatives. Companies whose employees are enthusiastic about diversity training and who complete the programs with flying colors may be more successful at fostering cultural competency than those whose employees eschew diversity training and fare poorly on trainer's evaluations. Experienced trainers often help companies identify potential obstacles in their path toward inclusion of people of color, people with disabilities, aging workers, women and GLBTs.

■ **Scorecards:** Scorecards can provide periodic reviews of a company's diversity efforts, examining progress at different segments. A scorecard may include numbers of employees of color, GLBTs, women, people with disabilities and other segments of employees at various levels of the company. Measurement also may be applied geographically, measuring the number of diverse employees compared to the

GLBT Metrics

The Human Rights Campaign Foundation's Corporate Equality Index gives companies a rating from zero to 100 percent in seven key areas of interest to gay, lesbian, bisexual and transgender (GLBT) employees, consumers and investors.[1] Some of the points of measurement also can be applied more generally as a means of benchmarking the success of diversity initiatives.

1. Include the words "sexual orientation" in their primary written nondiscrimination policy.

2. Include the words "gender identity" or "gender identity and/or expression" in their primary written nondiscrimination policy.

3. Offer health-insurance coverage to employees' same-sex domestic partners firm-wide; or provide cash compensation to employees to purchase health insurance for a domestic partner on their own.

4. Officially recognize and support a GLBT-employee resource group; or support employees' forming a GLBT-employee resource group if some expressed interest by providing space and other resources; or have a firm-wide diversity council or working group whose mission specifically includes GLBT diversity.

5. Offer diversity training that includes sexual orientation and/or gender identity and expression in the workplace.

6. Engage in respectful and appropriate marketing to the community and/or provide support through their corporate foundation or otherwise to GLBT health, educational, political or community organizations or events.

7. Engage in corporate action that would undermine the goal of equal rights for GLBTs.[2]

All companies are credited for No. 7 unless the organization has evidence that the company has engaged "in activities that undermine the goal of equal rights for GLBT people."[3]

population breakdown in a particular region, or by department, measuring the number of diverse employees by job function. Scorecards can be used to measure management success at achieving diversity initiatives as well.

■ **Management and employee evaluations:** Performance reviews and evaluations are excellent opportunities to determine whether programs, such as mentoring, employee-resource groups and other initiatives—which are put in place to foster diverse talent—are working. In addition, for managers whose compensation is tied to diversity goals and objectives, evaluations and reviews offer an opportunity to benchmark how well that manager is achieving diversity success.

■ **Exit interviews and post-employee surveys:** Employees may feel most at liberty to voice their concerns about a company's culture after they have left the company. Exit interviews and surveys of past employees can be excellent tools to uncover concerns about cultural competency. Schedule interviews with employees who have voluntarily left the company to determine the factors that contributed to their decisions to leave.

"You'll find out what may be on employees' minds, from the employees' point of view," says Redia Anderson, national principal, Diversity & Inclusion Initiative, Deloitte & Touche USA, during an interview for this book. "You can find out about complaints that are filed, if there are patterns around certain kinds of issues. We tend to think, 'Oh, it's only around discrimination,' but you may find that the company's benefit program doesn't align with needs of the current work force. Are there simple adjustments to be made there so that they're attracting the right talent that they need?"

> **"You'll find out what may be on employees' minds, from the employees' point of view."** - Redia Anderson

MEASURING CEO COMMITMENT

CEO commitment to diversity initiatives often isn't as clear-cut as measuring the number of people working in a specific job function. However, there are some methods of evaluating the support of C-level officers. A scorecard approach that measures the quantifiable issues and "grades" the CEO on the following issues can be a good way to apply metrics to the commitment level of the CEO:

■ **Accountability and incentive assessments:** How are employees held accountable for achievement of diversity initiatives? Regular reports should be submitted to the CEO, and managers should be held responsible, as part of their performance reviews, for achievement of diversity initiatives.

■ **Clear communication from the corner office:** Does the CEO regularly communicate the importance of diversity initiatives? How often do C-level senior managers incorporate the topic of diversity into their communications, both internally and externally?

It should be clear from the CEO's speeches, written correspondence, corporate mission and vision statements that diversity is a central part of the company's business operations. Similarly, does the company have clear and written nondiscrimination policies? Corporate leadership should make it clear that no employee will endure discrimination based on race/ethnicity, gender, sexual orientation, disability or age.

■ **Board diversity:** Is a culture of diversity evident at the highest levels of the company? If the board of directors does not include representation of women, people of color, people with disabilities or GLBTs, it may be more difficult for the CEO to communicate the importance of investing in the development of a diverse work force.

■ **Corporate commitment to fostering cultural competency:** Does the company invest and promote participation in programs that are designed to foster diverse employees? Mentoring programs, employee-resource groups and training are all important components of creating an environment where diverse employees feel welcome and have the resources they need to thrive. At what level does your organization support such programs?

■ **Employee benefits offerings:** Does the company invest in benefit programs that suit the needs of a diverse work force? Companies that are serious about diversity offer domestic-partner benefits, flexible work schedules and other programs designed to suit the needs of employees from different backgrounds, cultures and orientations.

■ **Who reports to the CEO:** The chief diversity officer or diversity director should be no more than one report away from the CEO. How many blacks, Latinos, Asian Americans, Native Americans, women, GLBTs or people with disabilities report directly to the CEO? If the CEO's direct reports are a diverse mix of different types of people, it's a good indication that the company is doing a good job of fostering a diverse culture.

■ **Involvement in diversity initiatives:** How involved is the CEO in diversity initiatives? Does she or he chair the company's diversity council? The most effective councils are chaired by the CEO or COO and meet on a regular basis, with solid levels of participation. The CEO should directly approve and review diversity objectives and progress, as well as be involved in analyzing solutions for programs that aren't yielding the desired results.

■ **Diversity-budget levels:** What is the size of the budget that the company has committed to diversity initiatives? Has that budget increased in recent years? As diversity initiatives continue to grow, they must be supported by appropriate corporate resources.

By evaluating these key activities and benchmarks, companies can get a clearer picture of the level of commitment to diversity at the C-level.

SUPPLIER-DIVERSITY MEASUREMENT

Metrics in supplier diversity can be measured readily. Dollar and percentage goals for spending with diverse suppliers are clear, as long as companies are willing to provide them.

Procurement software is a good way for companies to improve their supplier-diversity metrics. It allows them to accurately track their spending with diverse suppliers. In addition, it's important to adopt a uniform standard for reporting supplier-diversity spending that is equitable and transparent, including the creation of a substantive penalty for non-participation.

In 2005, the Top 10 Companies for Supplier Diversity were determined by several factors, including 10 new supplier-diversity questions. When measuring supplier diversity, it's important to make clear distinctions between spending with Tier I and Tier II women- and minority-owned businesses. DiversityInc asked whether Tier II supplier diversity was mandated and whether women- and minority-owned suppliers received third-party certification. In some cases, corporations include business with all small businesses—not just minority- and women-owned businesses—in their calculations of supplier diversity. We asked questions to clarify this point.[4]

Supplier diversity can be measured by both the number of businesses owned by women, people of color, and people with disabilities, as well as the percentage of spending with these companies, as compared with the company's total procurement budget. DiversityInc's Top 10 Companies for Supplier Diversity spent an average of 11.6 percent of their total procurement budgets with diverse suppliers, nearly double the 6.8 percent of the Top 50 and almost six times that of the national average of 2 percent. All require second-tier supplier diversity, which is 25 percent more than the Top 50 and 60 percent more than companies ranked 91 and higher.[5]

The National Minority Supplier Development Council (NMSDC) doesn't advocate setting a particular percentage goal for spending with diverse suppliers because that may lead to companies easing their commitment to diverse suppliers once they have hit a particular number, says Donna Long, vice president of development with the NMSDC. Instead, companies can measure their commitment to supplier diversity in several ways. Again, using a scorecard approach or other regular evaluation of the following factors can help you measure how your company's supplier-diversity program is performing.

■ **Certifications.** Does your supplier-diversity program require certification for Women-owned Business Enterprises (WBEs), Minority-owned Business Enterprises (MBEs) and businesses owned by people with disabilities? These third-party certifications ensure that suppliers truly fulfill the representations that they make to the corporations with which they do business.

■ **Numbers.** How many diverse suppliers versus suppliers overall does the company use? Examining the percentage of suppliers who are women, people of color and people with disabilities, and comparing them to the number of overall suppliers, can yield telling perspectives about where a supplier-diversity program may need to increase its outreach and pool of potential suppliers. Diverse-supplier calculations should not include small businesses in general but should include those businesses that have third-party MBE, WBE or owner-as-person-with-disability certification.

■ **Percentages.** What percentage of total procurement is spent with diverse suppliers? Here, it's important to look at a company's total spending and not just the percentage that may be earmarked for diverse suppliers. No sector of procurement should be excluded from supplier-diversity initiatives.

■ **Tier I Vs. Tier II.** Spending and percentage numbers can be misleading if spending and percentages of Tier I (primary supplier) and Tier II (secondary supplier or subcontractor) are not identified. When companies report their spending and diverse-supplier counts, those reports should indicate whether the spending is at the Tier I or Tier II level.

■ **Tier II Requirements.** Companies that are serious about supplier diversity often require it from their suppliers as well. Ensuring that diverse suppliers are, in turn, fostering supplier diversity in their operations ensures that larger corporations have a more sweeping impact on the development of MBEs, WBEs and businesses owned by people with disabilities, women, GLBTs, people of color and older Americans.

■ **Supplier-Diversity Resources.** To foster growth and success among diverse suppliers, larger companies often opt to provide development resources to those suppliers. These may include loans, mentoring programs, specialized training, payment terms or other methods of helping the supplier best service the corporation. Evaluating the number of and amount spent on resources to aid diverse suppliers are other good benchmarks of how committed a company is to its supplier-diversity program.

■ **Staffing.** The human capital devoted to supplier diversity is another means of measuring how committed a company is to supplier diversity. How many full-time employees are responsible for supplier diversity? In addition, such an analysis should take into consideration to whom those staffers report and whether supplier diversity is linked to procurement-management compensation.

Supplier-diversity metrics also may include whether the company has received recognition for supplier-diversity management, such as awards or publicity based on excellence in supplier diversity.

MARKETPLACE METRICS

Chapter 1 includes detail about the emerging and untapped markets of people of color, executive women, GLBTs, individuals with disabilities and older Americans. Clearly, companies that are poised to capitalize on those market trends will emerge with new opportunities for revenue growth. Later, Chapter 4 includes a checklist to help companies evaluate their outreach to both internal and external audiences. In order to effectively capture the attention and interest of these emerging and untapped markets, it's essential that corporate outreach, both internal and external, reflects the diversity objectives the company has set for itself. This can be measured in a variety of ways, including:

■ **Outreach audits**. Regularly review the company's methods of outreach, both internally and externally. Is diversity-related content regularly a part of corporate communication? Does the company have a statement of diversity in its mission, and do photographs and graphic images routinely feature people of color, women, workers of varying ages and people with disabilities?

■ **Online content.** Does the company's intranet feature information and resources for diverse workers? And does the corporate Web site include information about the company's commitment to diversity—including information about how diverse employees can apply to the company—no more than one click away from the homepage?

■ **Budget.** How much of the company's outreach budget is spent targeting diverse audiences? Companies should regularly evaluate the best opportunities for communicating to emerging and untapped markets and devote resources to multicultural marketing.

■ **Results.** Corporate investments should be measured by their return. Companies should use surveys, direct-response mechanisms and other market-research mechanisms to determine how outreach is impacting the perception of the company within the marketplace. In addition, sales figures should be analyzed to determine where the company's diversity outreach is having the most significant impact and where it can be improved.

■ Media mix. Marketing and corporate-communications departments should track spending and results in multicultural media as well as efforts to target multicultural audiences through mainstream media.

■ Multicultural-marketing resources. Does the marketing department have full-time employees dedicated to multicultural-marketing initiatives? Companies should evaluate the resources within marketing and corporate communications that are dedicated. The company should examine its communication points with customers and prospects and determine how it is ensuring that multicultural audiences are being served in direct selling, customer service and internal and external marketing.

■ Engagement of multicultural resources. Companies can often improve their outreach to diverse internal and external audiences by tapping their affinity groups and diversity council for input. Harnessing such diversity knowledge and applying it to existing efforts can create an additional facet to cultural competency. So, examine how frequently these groups are consulted about internal and external marketing efforts.

■ Recognition. Has the company been recognized or received publicity because of its commitment to diversity? External recognition is a good indicator that the company is making strong moves in creating an inclusive culture.

These measurement mechanisms will help your company ensure that its diversity efforts are being maximized through effective communication to core audiences. Because inclusive companies often benefit from positive word-of-mouth and enhanced reputations, effective communication of diversity efforts can help foster a greater awareness of the company's culture.

[1] Human Rights Foundation, "Corporate Equality Index 2004," page 6 http://www.hrc.org/ Template.cfm?Section= Corporate_Equality_ Index&Template=/ ContentManagement/ ContentDisplay.cfm& ContentID=23003

[2] Ibid

[3] Ibid

[4] *DiversityInc*, "Top 50 Companies for Diversity: Top 10 Companies for Supplier Diversity," June 2005, page 76

[5] Ibid

Like all corporate initiatives that yield results, creating an inclusive culture requires investment of resources, both financial and human. The exact proportion of those investments depends on the size of the company, its objectives, the level of commitment to the plan, the scope of the plan, and, ultimately, to the return on investment (ROI) that the plan shows. Companies that want a strong ROI on their diversity initiatives must invest in talented and motivated people and give them the necessary support to succeed. As previous chapters have outlined, these investments yield solid returns.

STARTING AT THE OUTCOME

When evaluating and funding a corporate-diversity initiative, companies need to look at the business case for diversity in that corporate environment. There are myriad demonstrable reasons for creating a culture of inclusion. What are the reasons that best support the company's objectives? They often include creating a wider and deeper pool of talent from which to draw employees; fostering a supplier base that will bring better value, stronger community ties and more options to the company; identifying and communicating to new market sectors to create a broader customer base; or many of the other excellent reasons from previous chapters.

CHAPTER 8

Diversity Return on Investments

It is critical to begin the diversity-planning process with a careful analysis of desired outcomes because that is the basis for the measurement and application of metrics discussed in Chapter 7. By defining the successful outcome, companies more effectively take the necessary steps to get there.

> ...creating an inclusive culture requires investment of resources, both financial and human.

Deloitte & Touche is very clear about its diversity and inclusion initiatives and what it expects to achieve from them, says Redia Anderson, national principal, Diversity & Inclusion Initiative, Deloitte & Touche USA. Deloitte & Touche is one of DiversityInc's 25 Noteworthy

Companies in 2005. The company's culture is closely tied to the corporate priority of having a pipeline of employee talent from which to draw. The company's diversity initiatives give it the ability to attract and retain the best employees, which contributes to the company's strong branding and marketplace recognition.

Whether a company is starting a diversity initiative from scratch or seeking to enhance its existing efforts, focusing on the desired outcomes is essential for success.

Whether a company is starting a diversity initiative from scratch or seeking to enhance its existing efforts, focusing on the desired outcomes is essential for success.

MAPPING THE ROUTE

Once the desired outcomes have been identified, the company needs to clearly outline the activities that must take place to accomplish those objectives. For instance, if the company seeks to create a more inclusive employee base, raising its employee population of people of color, older workers, GLBTs and people with disabilities by a certain percentage, it can:

■ Form employee-resource groups within the existing employee base to help brainstorm ideas and recruit a more diverse work force

■ Create alliances with professional associations, which help diverse candidates find jobs

■ Advertise in employment media, including magazines and Web sites, targeted toward diverse audiences

■ Participate in recruitment fairs and on-campus recruitment efforts and build strong relationships with colleges and universities that have diverse student populations

■ Update its Web site to include information about diversity and inclusion and job opportunities for diverse candidates

■ Institute employee surveys to determine which areas of corporate culture are more attractive to diverse candidates

■ Train employees in working within a more inclusive culture and institute financial rewards for those who succeed and a disciplinary process for those who fail

■ Tie management compensation to the achievement of diversity goals and objectives

By identifying the specific measurable outcome that is desired and creating a list of steps that need to be taken to accomplish those objectives, companies better plan the human and financial resources that will be necessary to achieve those objectives.

DIVERSITY DEPARTMENTS

Once the company has a clear understanding of its business reasons for creating an inclusive culture, it is essential to invest in the human capital necessary to take responsibility for carrying out the steps to achieve those outcomes. This responsibility often falls to a combination of a dedicated staff, existing employee base and, sometimes, external input from diversity experts, consultants or councils.

Typically, effective diversity initiatives are led by a core group of personnel headed by a diversity director or chief diversity officer. Companies on The DiversityInc Top 50 Companies for Diversity list usually structure their diversity departments so the head of the department either directly reports to the CEO or other C-level executive, or is no more than one report removed from that level. That level of prominence and access is essential for a successful effort.

In addition to the core staff responsible for diversity initiatives, the company should have a diversity council comprised of individuals who work in various capacities throughout the company, who are committed to the company's diversity efforts and who can bring insight and experience to helping the company move those initiatives forward.

In addition to the diversity council, the company should tap its employee base as part of the diversity effort in several ways. First and foremost, every employee needs to be properly trained in the company's policies on diversity and inclusion, with specialized training for managers whose compensation should be tied to diversity initiatives. Employee-resource groups are another excellent way to capture the input of diverse employees, including blacks, Latinos, Asian Americans, GLBTs, people with disabilities, and other employees who may benefit from peer-group support. These groups should be tapped for ideas for new policies and initiatives that will enhance the corporate culture as well as for ideas on new marketplace opportunities related to their knowledge of various market segments.

SETTING A BUDGET

We spoke with diversity directors from The 2005 DiversityInc Top 50 Companies for Diversity and found that diversity budgets are as varied as the companies that fund them, with annual budgets ranging from an average of $500,000 to $5 million.

The challenge in quantifying exactly how much diversity directors are spending on their efforts is that the money often is spread among different departments. So, while one company may include its supplier-diversity budget within its corporate-diversity department, another may have a smaller core of diversity professionals who work with human resources, purchasing, marketing and other operational functions to ensure that diversity objectives are achieved. In the latter case, the organization's diversity budget may seem smaller at first but actually is spread across several departments.

Diversity budgets are as varied as the companies that fund them, with annual budgets ranging from an average of $500,000 to $5 million

Depending on the structure of the company, line-item costs associated with diversity efforts also can vary greatly, based on factors such as identified outcomes, defined activities and number of staff members required to carry out the activities.

Following is a sample of the line items that could be included in such a budget. This is a composite of various budgets—no diversity director with whom we spoke had all of these areas within his or her budget. However, these figures represent a hypothetical annual budget, with a varying range for a company of approximately 10,000 employees. The numbers will vary based on objectives, corporate commitment to diversity and whether the entire budget is included in the diversity director's monetary allowance or if it is spread across several departments.

SAMPLE BUDGET:

COMPLIANCE AND HUMAN CAPITAL .... $200,000 to $1 million
Recruitment
    Recruitment-related travel
    Expos
    Recruitment advertising
    College relations
Employee-resource groups
    Meeting resources
Diversity-council-meeting expenses
Travel (peer-group meeting, for diversity-council members, etc.)
Mentoring programs
Consultant fees
Compliance training (legal issues, managing a diverse work force, etc.)
Online and in-person compliance education
Conferences

CORPORATE COMMUNICATIONS .... $120,000 to $3 million
Special events
Internal communication vehicles
    Publications
    Intranet
External communication vehicles
    Advertising
    Web site
    Public relations
General employee training

SUPPLIER DIVERSITY .... $100,000 to $750,000
Advertising in media targeted toward diverse suppliers
Supplier-database development, software
Organizational memberships to foster supplier diversity
Sponsorship of other events that attract diverse suppliers
Supplier-training programs

MEASUREMENT/ROI .... $25,000 to $500,000
Research, surveys, application of various metrics
to measure effectiveness of diversity initiatives and
determine where efforts need to be increased or improved.

REVENUE AND
SHAREHOLDER RETURN

With any corporate expenditure comes the responsibility of ensuring that the expenditure generates a ROI for the company. Since diversity has been wrongly perceived in the past as a "soft" initiative, it's even more crucial to its credibility that the financial value be proven.

Stock prices can fluctuate dramatically, especially when a company doesn't have a strong corporate image and the faith of the public. That faith in the management of a company is of utmost importance to a CEO. As we've seen in previous chapters, an examination of the stock performance of publicly traded companies on The DiversityInc Top 50 Companies for Diversity list reveals that strong diversity management is a clear signal that a company is well-managed and has long-term strength overall.[1]

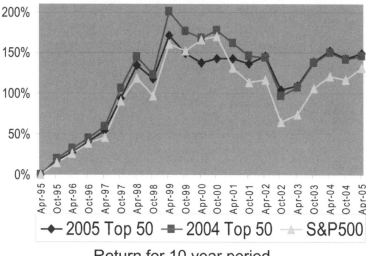

DiversityInc Top 50 Index

Return for 10-year period

◆ 2005 Top 50 ■ 2004 Top 50 ▲ S&P500

Strong diversity initiatives are the sign of a well-managed company, and that results in shareholder returns. Of The 2005 DiversityInc Top 50 Companies for Diversity, 43 companies are publicly traded. These 43 companies had a 23.5 percent higher return than the Standard & Poor's 500 when measured over 10 years with dividends reinvested.[2]

That speaks directly to long-term strength. And at the heart of that is the basic ingredient that makes a company run smoothly: people. Excellent diversity management means strong relationships with critical groups of people—employees, customers, suppliers and investors.

Diversity-management practices, when implemented properly, engage all of these stakeholders in using their personal background and development as it relates to the business of the company.[3]

In 2004, Cleveland, Ohio–based KeyBank (No. 13 on The 2005 DiversityInc Top 50 Companies for Diversity list) decided to further build its relationships with the 305 Native American tribes that live in the areas it serves. To lead the effort, KeyBank enlisted Mike Lettig, who is a Native American, as its Native American financial-services national executive. Lettig's understanding of tribal laws, governmental infrastructure and Native American cultures have been crucial to the program's success. Now KeyBank provides capital and financial services to more than 48 Native American tribes and corporations, with a total credit commitment of $488 million.[4]

For investors, that success sends the message that KeyBank is a company that markets to and attracts consumers of all social and economic levels, all races and all ethnicities. The bank's revenue streams, therefore, are less likely to dry up since it is continually building inroads to developing consumer markets.[5]

Catalyst, a nonprofit research and advisory organization for women in business, found that companies with the best representation of women within their management ranks also return the greatest value to shareholders and post the strongest return on equity.[6]

The 2004 study, entitled "The Bottom Line: Connecting Corporate Performance and Gender Diversity," examined gender diversity and financial performance and used two measures to examine financial performance: return on equity (ROE) and total return to shareholders (TRS). Out of 353 companies that were included among the Fortune 500 for four of five years between 1996 and 2000, ROE was 35 percent higher and TRS was 34 percent higher for companies with the strongest representation of women on executive-leadership teams, compared with companies with the lowest representation.[7]

While the study doesn't suggest that representation alone leads to bottom-line improvements, it underscores a fundamental principle of diversity: Companies with strong diversity strategies also are companies that have devised strong strategies to meet other challenges.[8]

PRODUCTIVITY

Because of the value and base of knowledge that diverse employees bring to a company, inclusive companies often benefit from an increase in productivity and an enhanced knowledge base in various issues. Tom Stevens, vice chairman of KeyBank, says diversity positively impacts the knowledge resources from which a company can draw.[9] "If you have diversity, you have a range of understanding about a particular issue," says Stevens. "We all have our own experiences and cultural and religious backgrounds, and we often don't recognize what we don't know. There's intellectual diversity, cultural, religious, race, gender, and when you bring those together, you get a better view of the scope of issues and a greater range of solutions."[10]

Companies that feature inclusive cultures will seek the best recruits from all walks of life as opposed to a select group from one walk of life. Featuring leadership, management and employees who bring with them different life experiences, knowledge of different consumer markets and different ideas on how to tackle business issues provides infinite possibilities for product and service development.[11]

NEW BUSINESS

In addition to helping companies leverage the value of their employees' experiences and knowledge to identify emerging and untapped markets for new business, companies more often are seeking out partners, suppliers and vendors who are committed to diversity and inclusion.

"Customers routinely ask about diversity initiatives," says Deloitte's Anderson. "We have many, many requests from clients and prospective clients asking us about our diversity and inclusion initiatives. 'What are you doing? What's working? What are your plans for the future?' We're seeing more and more clients asking those questions as a part of doing business with us and continuing their relationships."[12]

As companies seek out other companies with solid management practices, diversity initiatives are considered an excellent benchmark to determine those prospective partners.

REPORTING

Regular reporting also needs to be part of any company's diversity initiatives. Choosing the appropriate metrics for your company and its diversity goals, it's critical that the investments in diversity be quantified in their value to and impact on the company.

This also is why having senior management directly involved in diversity initiatives is essential. When the CEO or COO chairs the company's diversity council, for instance, he or she has a direct interest in evaluating the elements of the program that are working and growing those segments. Quantifying and reporting results becomes a much easier process because the senior-level management has direct involvement in the initiatives.

INVESTING IN THE FUTURE

Some companies believe that it's not enough to simply look at the immediate need for employees, or even a company's need a few years ahead. Deloitte works with INROADS, a nonprofit organization that places young people of color in business as interns, to help its talent pipeline.[13]

The company also drills further down than college, however. Deloitte has hundreds of employees working in high schools and middle schools through its Junior Achievement program. Employee participants speak with students about their experiences at Deloitte, career opportunities and broader concepts, such as what it means to be proficient in math and how it can help students in an accounting career.[14]

In response to the fast growth of the Latino population, Deloitte is forging relationships with Latino professionals in finance and accounting. As part of that initiative, the company is the host sponsor of the 2005 National Association of Latino Professionals in Finance and Accounting (ALPFA) convention. ALPFA is an organization of more than 2,000 Latino executives, professionals and students from accounting, finance and information technology. In addition, several Deloitte professionals are chapter presidents of local ALPFA chapters and have invested significant time and effort supporting the involvement of more Latino professionals in finance and accounting.[15]

THE BOTTOM LINE

Measurement, return, reporting and results: While they aren't always the first things that come to mind when companies are considering diversity initiatives, they are critical components of such programs.

By defining clear desired outcomes from the start, companies seeking a more inclusive culture have concrete, business-focused reasons for doing so.

There are many ways to quantify the results of diversity initiatives, as we saw in Chapter 7, but those methods should be chosen according to which will best measure the results that are tied to the desired outcomes. Anderson counsels companies to always look at the bigger picture, however.

"There often is not a one-to-one correlation—because you've got diversity and inclusion, you've got X," she explains. "There are a number of factors that figure in, such as talent, skills, knowledge, all of those benefit the company and factored in as part of diversity and inclusion. That's another indication that we have that there is a bottom-line impact."

[1] DiversityInc.com, "How Diversity Impacts Shareholder Return", by Yoji Cole, June 14, 2005

[2] Ibid

[3] Ibid

[4] Ibid

[5] Ibid

[6] DiversityInc.com, "More Women Managers Yield Better Financial Performance," by Linda Bean, January 27, 2004

[7] Ibid

[8] Ibid

[9] DiversityInc.com, "How Diversity Impacts Shareholder Return", by Yoji Cole, June 14, 2005

[10] Ibid

[11] Ibid

[12] Interview with Anderson

[13] Ibid

[14] Ibid

[15] Statement from Deloitte, released August 8, 2005

As the demographics in the United States continue to shift, companies that have put effective diversity initiatives in place will reap the benefits. As we've seen in the preceding chapters, those benefits can be significant, from tapping emerging markets to attracting and retaining better talent to saving money to increasing profits and creativity.

Through our work reporting on the latest news, developments and best practices in corporate diversity, and the information aggregated through the annual DiversityInc Top 50 Companies for Diversity list, DiversityInc educates companies on the business benefits of diversity. Senior management and corporate leaders who are serious about the effective management of their companies need to build a diversity program based on the four cornerstones that are the basis of every effective diversity initiative: human capital, CEO commitment, corporate communications and supplier diversity.

The structure that is built upon those cornerstones varies greatly from company to company. Some companies have dedicated departments that handle myriad diversity responsibilities, while others

Conclusion

have a small core of diversity professionals who work throughout the company to create positive change. Through the Top 50 data, however, DiversityInc sees some of the common threads among the most successful companies, including a diversity chief who is no more than one report removed from the CEO level, a diversity council headed by the CEO, an emphasis placed on employee recruitment and retention, support for diverse suppliers to enable them to grow as they serve their clients, and inclusive outreach to both internal and external audiences. Following the examples set by the Top 50 is the most effective way to improve cultural competency.

We expect measurement of these programs and policies to continue to be a priority for well-managed companies in the years ahead. As measurement becomes more widespread and universal in nature, those benchmarks increasingly will show the financial rewards of an inclusive corporate culture.

Going forward, diversity will affect every area of business as the increasingly significant return on investment is calculated. Companies are continuing to track and measure how every dollar spent on inclusive practices in talent recruitment, marketing, employee retention, supplier development, and other diversity initiatives influences the bottom line. As we've shown in this fifth edition of *The Business Case for Diversity*, more companies are looking at the hard numbers and realizing that the future of their companies depends on the success of their diversity initiatives.

Able-bodied: Refers to a person who does not have a disability. Although not a derogatory term, it is not preferred. Use *non-disabled*.

Acculturation: Process of acquiring a second culture. It is not *assimilation*.

ADA: Acronym for *Americans with Disabilities Act*, federal civil-rights legislation that deals with discrimination in employment, public accommodations, transportation and telecommunications on the basis of disability. Spell out in full upon first reference.

Affirmative action: Describes concept upheld by the Supreme Court that allows universities to consider race, ethnicity and gender for admissions with the goal of alleviating past inequities. Also can be used to describe similar programs used by businesses and other organizations. Do not use *quota system* or *reverse discrimination* as substitute phrases except in quotes.

African American: Person of color and of African-slave descent from the United States. Hyphenate only when used as an adjective.

Alien: Used by federal government to describe a foreign-born U.S. resident who is not a citizen. Those who enter the United States legally are *resident aliens* and are issued *alien registration cards*, known as green cards because they once were green. Those who reside in

Glossary

the United States illegally are classified as *illegal aliens*. Avoid these terms outside of a legal context because many people consider them derogatory. Use either *legal immigrant* or *legal resident* instead of *resident alien*. Use either *illegal immigrant* or *undocumented immigrant* instead of *illegal alien*.

American: Describes a citizen of the United States. However, the term may also describe any citizen of North, Central or South America.

American Indian: Used by the U.S. Census Bureau as the preferred term for Native American. Although not a derogatory term, and used by some Native Americans, it is not preferred. Do not use *Indian* as a synonym.

American Sign Language: the most common language used by deaf people in North America. See *ASL*.

Americans with Disabilities Act: See *ADA*.

Arab: Person from an Arabic-speaking nation. Not a synonym for Muslim. Most Arabs are Muslim, but not all Muslims are Arab (e.g. Iranians are Persian and speak Farsi).

Asian: Describes a resident of the continent of Asia, regardless of race or ethnicity. Not a synonym for *Asian American*.

Asian American: Person of Asian descent from the United States. Hyphenate only when used as an adjective. *Asian* is not a synonym.

ASL: Acronym for *American Sign Language*, the most common language used by deaf people in North America.

Assimilation: Process of replacing one's first culture with a second culture. It is not *acculturation*.

Baby boomer: A person born between 1946 and 1964.

Bilingual: Although bilingual often refers to Spanish and English, it describes fluency between any two languages.

Bindi: Hindi name for decoration worn by some Indian women between the eyebrows. Does not indicate marital status.

Bisexual: Person attracted to either sex, as well as the sexual and emotional attraction to either sex. Do not assume or infer non-monogamy.

Bicultural: A person who identifies with two cultures.

Biracial: A person who identifies with two races.

Black: Person of color of African descent, regardless of national origin.

Board of directors: A group of advisers who oversee the governance of a corporation.

Caucasian: Synonym for white person. Use *white* unless Caucasian is in a quote or title.

Civil rights: Political, social and economic legal rights and responsibilities guaranteed by the government. Also *equal rights*. Many groups in U.S. history, such as women, people of color and GLBTs, have struggled to attain them. The *civil-rights movement* refers to the struggles of African Americans. Do not use *special rights*.

Civil union: Legal recognition of same-sex couples, first established in Vermont, that provides many of the legal rights of married couples. Civil unions are not marriages or *domestic partnerships*. Many politicians have proposed civil unions as an alternative to gay marriage.

Closeted: Describes a person who does not want to reveal his or her own *sexual orientation* or *gender identity*. Also, *in the closet*.

Colored: Although used in regions of Africa to describe people of mixed race, do not use in the United States to refer to *people of color*.

Coming out: Abbreviated form of *coming out of the closet*. Choosing to reveal formerly hidden *sexual orientation* or *gender identity*.

Corporate communications: The process by which a company relays information and messages to key audiences and stakeholders.

Derogatory terms: Offensive words or phrases. Do not use except in quotes that reveal the bias of people quoted or when their use is in some way essential to a written communication. Terms considered derogatory by many people are used by some people in an informal, non-derogatory manner among each other in an attempt to reclaim them from their hateful origins. Because such usage is controversial, however, and people who use these terms informally consider their use by people not in their group as inappropriate, avoid them.

Disability: Functional limitation of at least one major life activity, such as walking, learning, etc. Legal definitions vary. Do not mention unless relevant. *Person with a disability* is preferred, not *disabled person*. Do not use *victim of, suffers from, stricken with, afflicted with*.

Disabled: Do not use *the disabled*. Use *people with disabilities, disability community*, or *disability activists* as alternatives.

Discrimination: Unfair treatment of a group based on a prejudice against that group or a preference for another group. May relate to race/ethnicity, gender, sexual orientation, age or other factors.

Diversity: Although often related to only *race, ethnicity* and *gender*, it also includes *people with disabilities, sexual orientation* and *gender identity*, and *age*. White people should be included.

Domestic partnership: Legal recognition of unmarried, *opposite-sex couples* and *same-sex couples*, which gives them some of the same rights as married couples. *Domestic partnerships* are not *marriages* or *civil unions*. They are not usually binding between jurisdictions.

EEOC: Acronym for *Equal Employment Opportunity Commission*, a federal agency that enforces all civil-rights laws.

Emerging market: A potential base of customers that is growing in numbers and viability.

Emigrant: Person who exits a country of origin to live elsewhere.

ESL: Acronym for *English as a Second Language*, a method of teaching English in the United States to non-English speakers.

Ethnicity: Classification of humans based on shared cultural heritage, such as place of birth, language, customs, etc. Do not use *race* as a synonym.

Foreign-born: An individual born in a country other than the one in which he or she currently resides.

Gay: Person attracted to the same sex, sexually and emotionally. Most associated with gay men. Describes *gay men, lesbians, bisexuals* and *transgender people* as a group, but the acronym *GLBT* is preferred.

Gay marriage: Marriage for same-sex couples. Also *same-sex marriage*. Use *marriage for same-sex couples* when possible.

Gender: Masculine or feminine, regardless of sex. Do not use sex as a synonym.

Gender-neutral terms: In general, use gender-neutral terms (e.g. *police officer*, not *policeman*) whenever possible, except if gender-specific terms are preferred by the person or if in a quote or title.

Gender expression: Describes how *gender identity* is expressed, regardless of *sexual orientation*, including traditionally masculine or feminine behavior, clothing, hairstyles, voice and gestures.

Gender identity: Self-identification as male or female, regardless of sex assigned at birth. Do not use *gender identity* and *sexual orientation* as synonyms.

GLBT: Acronym for *gay, lesbian, bisexual and transgender*. Also *LGBT*. Although *LGBT(s)* is widely used, *GLBT(s)* is still preferred by most sources. Many gay activists consider *GLBT* and *LGBT* to be more inclusive than *gay* as an adjective. Always use *gay, lesbian, bisexual and transgender* on first reference.

Handicap, handicapped: Although they are not derogatory terms, avoid them when possible. Use only in legal contexts, in quotes or titles. Use *disability, disabled*.

HBCU: Acronym for *historically black colleges and universities*, established to provide higher education to blacks at a time in U.S. history when such access was limited. Most of them now do not have only blacks as students, but most of them still retain black majorities.

Hermaphrodite: Derogatory term for intersex person. Derived from *hermaphroditism*, a medical term.

Heterosexual: Person attracted to the opposite sex, sexually and emotionally. Use *straight* only in informal contexts.

Hindi: Official language of India. Not synonymous with *Hindu*, an adherent of *Hinduism*.

Hinduism: Major religion of India. Not synonymous with *Hindi*, the official language of India.

Hip hop: An urban culture rooted in rap music, breakdancing and graffiti that was created by blacks and Latinos in the late 1970s, now popular with U.S. youth. Do not capitalize. Hyphenated only when used as an adjective.

Hispanic: Person of descent from a Spanish-speaking country, regardless of ability to speak *Spanish*. Always capitalized. Use *Latino* instead of *Hispanic*, except if the person prefers Hispanic, if Hispanic is in a quote or title, or if Latino would be inaccurate.

Homophobia: Describes fear, hatred and/or dislike of *gay men* and *lesbians*. Also often includes *bisexuals* and *transgender people*, but *transphobia* is the term when referring to *transgender* people specifically.

Homosexual: Person attracted to the same sex, sexually and emotionally. Because of negative use historically, avoid *homosexual* as a synonym for gay. Use only if *heterosexual* would be used similarly, such as in scientific reference.

HSI: Acronym for *Hispanic-serving institutions*, a term created by the federal government. HSIs must have at least 25 percent Latinos, half of which are low-income. Universities that earn this classification become eligible for additional funding.

Hyphenated Americans: Derogatory term coined by Theodore Roosevelt to describe Americans who he believed did not want to join the U.S. mainstream. Still used negatively to describe people who identify as African American, Mexican American, etc., even though these terms are now hyphenated only when used as adjectives.

Immigrant: Person who enters a new country to live. Also emigrant.

Immigration: Avoid negative related terms such as *invasion*. Use neutral terms such as *arrival*.

Inclusive: Refers to a workplace in which people from a variety of races/ethnicities, genders, ages, abilities, sexual orientations and backgrounds are welcome.

In-culture: Describes outreach to racial and ethnic groups using familiar cultural contexts, which can include methods, images and language.

In-language: Describes outreach to racial and ethnic groups in their native languages.

Indigenous: Describes descendants of native people of any region. Use specific terms whenever possible, such as *Native Americans, Inuit*, etc.

Intersex: Person whose sex is ambiguous. Intersex people are often operated on soon after birth, but it is becoming more common not to perform surgery, even though a sex is assigned. In these cases, intersex people are allowed to make their own decisions about their sex and whether to have surgery when their gender identities are more apparent. Use pronoun preferred by the intersex person. Do not assume *gender identity* or *sexual orientation*. Do not use *hermaphrodite*.

Invalid: Derogatory term for person with a disability.

Islam: Religion founded by Muhammad. *Muslims* are adherents of Islam. *Islam* and *Muslim* are not synonyms. An *imam* is a leader of prayer at a *mosque*, an Islamic place of worship. The two major divisions are *Sunni* and *Shiite*. Most Islamic countries have Sunni majorities, except Iran, which has a Shiite majority.

Jihad: Describes a war against any unjust regime, but only to be waged against the leaders, not the people. Islam does not sanction any other definition.

Judaism: Religion founded by Abraham and Moses. Adherents are *Jews*; also, *Hebrews*. Jews can be of any race or nationality. *Hebrew* is the official language of Israel, which has a secular government. Both *Christians* and *Muslims* also trace their religious heritage back to Abraham. Do not use *kike, hebe* or *heeb*, which most Jews consider extremely derogatory.

Latin America: In common usage, includes all countries in the Americas that are primarily Spanish- and Portuguese-speaking. Although French-speaking countries are sometimes included in this definition, such usage is not preferred.

Latino: Person of Latin American descent, regardless of ability to speak Spanish or Portuguese. Always capitalized. Always use *Latino* instead of *Hispanic*, except if the person prefers *Hispanic*, if *Hispanic* is in a quote or title, or if it would be more accurate. Also, *Latina(s)* for women and *Latino(s)* for women and men in a group. The U.S. Census Bureau limits the term to people of descent from Spanish-speaking countries.

Lesbian: Woman attracted to other women, sexually and emotionally. *Gay* also is sometimes used.

LGBT: *See GLBT.*

Little people: Describes people of short stature. Derived from *Little People of America*, an advocacy group. Although used by some people of short stature, use *people of short stature*.

MBE: Acronym for *Minority Business Enterprise*. Also, *minority-owned business*. MBE certification by federal or local government allows companies to compete for certain business.

Marginalize: To dismiss as unimportant or irrelevant.

Mental illness: Describes diseases of the mind, such as depression, anxiety, schizophrenia, etc. Do not use derogatory terms such as *loony, nuts, crazy, insane*, etc. Do not use *mental* by itself to describe a person.

Mestizo: Although used by many Latin Americans and Latinos to describe a person of mixed Spanish and indigenous descent, avoid unless in a quote or in a title.

Metrics: Methods of measuring various aspects of a company.

Midget: Derogatory term for a *person of short stature*.

Migrant: Although *migrant* can be defined as a person who migrates, the term mostly refers to farm laborers who move often to different locations to harvest seasonal crops. Do not use as a synonym for *immigrant* or *emigrant*.

Minority: Describes person/group not in the majority. Historically refers to *people of color*, but can describe other groups, such as women, depending on the context. Use only when part of a quote or title. Use *people of color* or other specific terms when possible, such as *black, Latino*, etc.

Mission statement: A company's written assertion of its core values and reason for being.

MTF: Acronym for male-to-female. Describes *transgender* person classified as male at birth but who also identifies as female. Do not assume *sex reassignment surgery*.

Muhammad: Founder of Islam. Do not use alternate spellings unless preferred by people for their own proper names or as used by Muslims in titles or phrases.

Muslim: Adherent of Islam. Adherents of a U.S. Islamic sect of mostly blacks consider themselves Muslims. Do not call them *Black Muslims*.

Multicultural: Referring to something that represents different races/ethnicities, religions and other backgrounds and orientations.

Native American: Descendent of the native inhabitants of the United States, regardless of tribal affiliation. *American Indian* is used by U.S. Census Bureau, but *Native American* is preferred. *Indian* is not a synonym. Do not use *half-blood* or *half-breed*, derogatory terms for a Native American of mixed racial and ethnic heritage.

Native-born: Describes a person in the United States. Does not refer specifically to a Native American.

Negro: Once considered appropriate, this term for *black people* and *African Americans* is outdated. Do not use except when part of a title or phrase as used by blacks.

Nigger: Derogatory term for *black people* and *African Americans*. Because it continues to be extremely offensive to many *people of color*, do not use it except in very rare circumstances, even in quotes. Do not confuse with *niggard* (a miser) or *niggardly* (miserly).

Non-disabled: Preferred term for a person without a disability. Although not derogatory, avoid *able-bodied*.

Ñ: Do not substitute n for this 17th letter of the 29-letter Spanish alphabet. [For PC users, press Ctrl plus Shift plus ~ then hold and press n for Ñ (uppercase); press Ctrl plus Shift plus ~ then release and press n for ñ (lowercase)].

Opposite-sex couples: Describes couples with partners of the opposite sex. Although heterosexuality is implied, this term also includes couples where one or both partners are bisexual. Hyphenate *opposite-sex* only when used as an adjective.

Oriental: Derogatory term for Asian and Asian American.

Outing: Also *to out*. Describes revealing *sexual orientation* or *gender identity*.

Pacific Islander: Used by U.S. Census Bureau to describe people from Fiji, Guam, Hawaii, Northern Mariana Islands, Palau, Samoa, Tahiti and Tonga. Also used by many Asian Americans and Pacific Islanders for people from the Pacific Islands in general, but use specific countries when possible.

Pacific Rim: Describes imaginary line that frames the Pacific Ocean, which borders several countries, primarily the United States, Canada, China, Japan and Australia. Not derogatory, but use specific regions and countries when possible.

Paraplegia: Paralysis of the legs and often other parts of the lower half of the body, usually due to spinal-cord damage.

Partner: Describes person in an *opposite-sex couple* or a *same-sex couple* who usually is unmarried. Use *girlfriend, boyfriend, lover* or *companion* if the couple prefers those terms. Use *partner* if they prefer it or if their preference is unknown.

People of color: Describes all people who are not white. Also *person of color*. When describing a title or geographic location, *of color* can be used alone (e.g. *directors of color, New Yorker of color*). Use specific terms (*blacks, Latinos, Asian Americans*) when possible.

Person of short stature: See *short stature*.

Quadriplegia: Disability where a person physically can neither use his or her legs nor arms.

Queer: Derogatory term for *gay*. Although queer has become acceptable among some GLBTs as an inclusive alternative for *gay* or *GLBT*, it is still considered offensive by many GLBTs because of its negative history. Do not use it unless part of a quote, title or phrase used by GLBTs.

Quran: Muslim holy book. Also *Koran*. Always use *Quran* except if *Koran* is part of a title.

Race: Classification of humans based on genetic characteristics, such as skin color, hair, facial features, etc. Not synonymous with *ethnicity*.

Rap: Predominant genre of music in *hip hop*.

Recruitment: The process of attracting employees to a company.

Religious terms: Do not use *fundamentalist* or *liberal* unless preferred by groups or individuals. Use *conservative* or *moderate*, respectively, as alternates. Avoid *Judeo-Christian*.

Retention: When used to refer to employees, the number of employees that remain employed by a company because both the employee and the employer agree to that employment.

Same-sex couples: Describes couples with *partners* of the same sex. Although homosexuality is implied, this term includes couples in which one or both partners are *bisexual*. Hyphenate *same-sex* only when used as an adjective.

Second-tier supplier: An individual or company that provides products or services to a company that is a primary provider of products or services to a (usually larger) company. Many inclusive companies require their vendors to cultivate diversity among their suppliers.

Sex: Physical distinction between male and female, regardless of gender. Do not use *gender* as a synonym.

Sexual orientation: Describes sexual and emotional attraction, such as *homosexual* (gay or lesbian), *bisexual* and *heterosexual*. Not synonymous with *gender identity* or *gender expression*.

Short stature: Preferred term instead of *little people*. Do not use *dwarf* or *midget*, which are both derogatory terms.

Spanglish: Slang combination of Spanish with English. Not a language or dialect. Do not use in print.

Spanish: Describes primary language spoke in Spain and most of Latin America. Also describes a person from Spain. Do not use as a synonym for *Latino* or *Hispanic*.

Special rights: Derogatory term for *civil rights* and *equal rights*.

Spic: Derogatory term for *Latino* and *Hispanic*.

Straight: Heterosexual.

Stereotype: Generalizations, often derogatory, about groups based on opinions, exaggerations or distorted assertions.

Stutterer: Not preferred. Use *person who stutters*.

Suppliers: Companies that provide products or services to other companies.

Supplier diversity: The effort among many companies to purchase products and services from companies owned by diverse individuals.

Tejano: Person from Texas of Mexican descent.

Third World: Used during the Cold War, it describes countries in Africa, Asia and Latin America still developing economically. Do not use except in quotes or in a title. The term *developing countries* is preferred.

TOEFL: Acronym for *Teaching of English as a Foreign Language*, a method of teaching English in other countries to non-English speakers.

Transgender: Person whose *gender identity* and/or *gender expression* varies from the sex assigned at birth. Describes *transsexuals, cross-dressers, intersex people* and many other classifications. *Sexual orientation* is not to be assumed. Use a specific term when known or if preferred by the person. Use *transgender* when a specific term is not known or if preferred by the person. Do not use *transgendered*.

Transition: Process of altering *sex* to match self-identified *gender*, which can include hormone therapy, sex-reassignment surgery and/or legal identity.

Transsexual: Person who identifies as a member of the opposite sex, regardless of *sexual orientation*. A transsexual may or may not choose to undergo physical alterations, up to and including *sex-reassignment surgery*, which is the preferred term for *sex-change operation*. *Sexual orientation* is not to be assumed. Use the pronoun that matches public appearance and/or that is preferred by the person. Do not use transsexual as a synonym for *transgender*.

Transvestite: Derogatory term for a *transsexual* or a *transgender* person.

Tribe: Although not derogatory, avoid except in quotes or a title, or when modified into an adjective (e.g. tribal law). Many Native Americans prefer *nation*. Avoid referring to ethnic groups in Africa (e.g. Hutu, Tutsi, etc.) as tribes.

Unacculturated: One who has not accepted a new culture.

WBE: Acronym for *Women's Business Enterprise*. Also *woman-owned business*. WBE certification by the federal or local government allows companies to compete for certain business.

Wheelchair: Use *wheelchair-user* or *person who uses a wheelchair*. Do not use *wheelchair-bound* or *confined to a wheelchair*. Do not use unless relevant.

White: Defined by the U.S. Census Bureau as a person of descent from the original peoples of Europe, the Middle East and North Africa.

DEMOGRAPHIC RESEARCH

American Association of Retired Persons (AARP)

http://www.aarp.org/
601 E Street, N.W.
Washington, DC 20049
Telephone: (800) 687-2277

American Association of People with Disabilities

http://www.aapd-dc.org/
1629 K Street, N.W.
Suite 503
Washington, DC 20006
Telephone: (202) 457-0046
(800) 840-8844

Resources

Bureau of Labor Statistics

http://www.bls.gov
Division of Information Services
2 Massachusetts Avenue, N.E.
Room 2860
Washington, DC 20212
Telephone: (202) 691-5200
Fax: (202) 691-7890
TDD: (202) 691-5200
(800) 877-8339

Community Marketing, Inc.

http://www.communitymarketinginc.com/index.cfm
584 Castro Street
Suite 834
San Francisco, CA 94114-2594
Telephone: (415) 437-3800
Fax: (415) 552-5104

Human Rights Campaign Foundation

http://www.hrc.org/
1640 Rhode Island Avenue, N.W.
Washington, DC 20036-3278
Front Desk: (202) 628-4160
Fax: (202) 347-5323
TTY: (202) 216-1572
(800) 727-4723

National Organization on Disability

http://www.nod.org/
910 Sixteenth Street, N.W.
Suite 600
Washington, DC 20006
Telephone: (202) 293-5960
Fax: (202) 293-7999
TTY: (202) 293-5968

Selig Center For Economic Growth

http://www.selig.uga.edu
Terry College of Business
The University of Georgia
Athens, GA 30602-6269
Telephone: (706) 425-2962

U.S. Census Bureau

http://www.census.gov/
DC Address:
U.S. Census Bureau
4700 Silver Hill Road
Washington, DC 20233-0001

Telephone Centers:
Hagerstown Address:
U.S. Census Bureau
Hagerstown Telephone Center
1125 Opal Court
2nd Floor
Hagerstown, MD 21740
Telephone: (240) 420-6020

Fax: (240) 420-6033
(800) 321-1995

Jeffersonville Address:
U.S. Census Bureau
Jeffersonville Telephone Center
1201 E. 10th Street
Jeffersonville, IN 47132
Telephone: (812) 218-4100
Fax: (812) 218-4266
TDD: (812) 218-4316
(800) 582-8330

Tucson Address:
U.S. Census Bureau
Tucson Telephone Center
201 N. Bonita Avenue
Suite 125
Tucson, AZ 85745
Telephone: (520) 798-4160
Fax: (520) 798-4164
TDD: (520) 798-4150
(800) 786-9448

HUMAN CAPITAL

Advanced Internet Recruiting Strategies (AIRS)
http://www.airsdirectory.com
58 Fogg Farm Road
White River Junction, VT 05001
Telephone: (800) 897-7714
Fax: (888) 997-5559

Employee Benefit Research Institute (EBRI)
http://www.ebri.org
2121 K Street, N.W.
Suite 600
Washington, DC 20037-1896
Telephone: (202) 659-0670
Fax: (202) 775-6312

U.S. Equal Employment Opportunity Commission
http://www.eeoc.gov
1801 L Street, N.W.
Suite 100
Washington, DC 20507
Telephone: (202) 663-4900
Fax: (202) 663-4912

Human Resource Planning Society (HRPS)
http://www.hrps.org
317 Madison Avenue
Suite 1509
New York, NY 10017
Telephone: (212) 490-6387
Fax: (212) 682-6851

Society for Human Resource Management
http://www.shrm.org/
1800 Duke Street
Alexandria, VA 22314
Telephone: (703) 548-3440
TTY/TTD: (703) 548-6999
Fax: (703) 535-6490
(800) 283-7476

STUDENT ORGANIZATIONS FOR RECRUITMENT

HBCUConnect.com
http://www.hbcuconnect.com
5300 E. Main St., Suite 107
Columbus, OH 43213
Telephone: (614) 284-3007
Fax: (215) 893-5398

Hispanic Alliance for Career Enhancement (HACE)
http://www.hace-usa.org
25 E. Washington St.
Suite 1500
Chicago, IL 60602

Telephone: (312) 435-0498
Fax: (312) 435-1494

INROADS
http://www.inroads.org/
10 South S. Broadway
Suite 300
St. Louis, MS 63102
Telephone: (314) 241-7488
Fax: (314) 241-9325

Jackie Robinson Foundation
http://www.jackierobinson.org/
3 W. 35th Street
11th Floor
New York, NY 10001
Telephone: (212) 290-8600
Fax: (212) 290-8081

Leadership Education and Development (LEAD)
http://www.leadprogram.org
14 E. Hartwell Lane
Philadelphia, PA 19118
Telephone: (215) 753-2490

**National Association for Equal Opportunity
in Higher Education (NAFEO)**
http://www.nafeo.org
Main Office
8701 Georgia Avenue
Suite 200
Silver Spring, MD 20910
Telephone: (301) 650-2440
Fax: (301) 495-3306

Executive Office
1090 Vermont Ave, N.W.
Suite 800
Washington D.C. 20005
Telephone: (202) 558-3544

The PhD Project
http://www.phdproject.org
3 Chestnut Ridge Road
Montvale, NJ 07645
Telephone: 1-888-2GET-APHD

Thurgood Marshall Scholarship Fund
http://www.thurgoodmarshallfund.org/
90 William Street
Suite 1203
New York, NY 10038
Telephone: (212) 573-8888
Fax: (212) 573-8497

Historically Black Colleges and Universities
A list of historically black colleges and universities and links to their
Web sites:
http://www.smart.net/~pope/hbcu/hbculist.htm

Historically Hispanic Colleges and Universities
A list of historically Hispanic college and universities and links to their
Web sites:
http://www.chci.org/chciyouth/resources/hispanicserving.htm

SUPPLIER DIVERSITY

Association for Service Disabled Veterans
http://www.asdv.org/
110 Maryland Avenue, N.E. – Suite 100
Washington, DC 20002
Telephone: (202) 543-1942
Fax: (202) 543-5398

National Minority Business Council
http://www.nmbc.org
25 W. 45th Street
Suite 301
New York, NY 10036
Telephone: (212) 997-4753
Fax: (212) 997-5102

National Minority Supplier Development Council, Inc. (NMSDC)

http://www.nmsdcus.org/index.html
1040 Avenue of the Americas
2nd Floor
New York, NY 10018
Telephone: (212) 944-2430
Fax: (212) 719-9611

National Women Business Owners Corporation

http://www.nwboc.org
1001 W. Jasmine Drive – Suite G
Lake Park, FL 33403
Telephone: (800) 675-5066
Fax: (561) 881-7364

Small Business Administration

http://www.sba.gov
740 15th Street, N.W.
3rd Floor
Washington, DC 20005-3544
Telephone: (202) 272-0345
Fax: (202) 272-0344

Women's Business Enterprise National Council

http://www.wbenc.org
1120 Connecticut Avenue, N.W. – Suite 1000
Washington, DC 20036
Telephone: (202) 872-5515 ext. 10
Fax: (202) 872-5505

CORPORATE COMMUNICATIONS

American Association of Advertising Agencies

http://www.aaaa.org
405 Lexington Avenue
18th Floor
New York, NY 10174-1801
Telephone: (212) 682-2500
Fax: (212) 682-8391

Association of Hispanic Advertising Agencies

http://www.ahaa.org
8201 Greensboro Drive
3rd Floor
McLean, VA 22102
Telephone: (703) 610-9014
Fax: (703) 610-9005

Latinos in Information Sciences and Technology Association (LISTA)

http://www.aramwebs.com/lista
92 Van Cortlandt Park South
Suite #6a
Riverdale NY 10463
Telephone: (347) 632-4542

Multicultural Marketing Resources

http://www.multicultural.com
286 Spring Street
Suite 201
New York, NY 10013
Telephone: (212) 242-3351
Fax: (212) 691-5969

National Association for Multi-ethnicity in Communications (NAMIC)

http://www.namic.com
336 W. 37th Street
Suite 302
New York, NY 10018
Telephone: (212) 594-5985
Fax: (212) 594-8391

ADVOCACY GROUPS

ASIAN AMERICAN RESOURCES

Committee of 100

http://www.committee100.org

677 Fifth Avenue
5th Floor
New York, NY 10022
Telephone: (212) 371-6565
Fax: (212) 371-9009

National Association of Asian American Professionals
http://www.naaap.org
P.O. Box 52030
Boston, MA 02205
Telephone: (773) 918-2454

Organization of Chinese Americans
http://www.ocanatl.org
1001 Connecticut Avenue, N.W.
Suite 601
Washington, DC 20036
Telephone: (202) 223-5500
Fax: (202) 296-0540

Japanese American Citizens League
http://www.jacl.org
1765 Sutter Street
San Francisco, CA 94115
Telephone: (415) 921-5225

Korean American Coalition
http://www.kacla.org
3421 W. 8th Street
2nd Floor
Los Angeles, CA 90005
Telephone: (213) 365-5999

Asian American Justice Center
http://www.advancingequality.org
1140 Connecticut Avenue, N.W.
Suite 1200
Washington, DC 20036
Telephone: (202) 296-2300
Fax: (202) 296-2318

Asian Women in Business

http://www.awib.org
358 Fifth Avenue
Suite 504
New York, NY 10001
Telephone: (212) 868-1368
Fax: (212) 868-1373

BLACK RESOURCES

NAACP Legal Defense and Educational Fund

http://www.naacpldf.org
New York Office
99 Hudson Street
Suite 1600
New York, NY 10013
Telephone: 212-965-2200

Washington, D.C. Office
1444 I Street, N.W.
Washington, DC 20005
Telephone: (202) 682-1300

Western Regional Office
1055 Wilshire Boulevard
Suite 1480
Los Angeles, CA 90017
Telephone: (213) 975-0211

National Urban League

http://www.nul.org
120 Wall Street
8th Floor
New York, NY 10005
Telephone: (212) 558-5300

National Association for the Advancement of Colored People

http://www.naacp.org
The NAACP Legal Department

4805 Mt. Hope Drive
Baltimore, MD 21215
Telephone: (410) 580-5790

Rainbow/PUSH Coalition
http://www.rainbowpush.org
930 E. 50th Street
Chicago, IL 60615-2702
Telephone: (773) 373-3366
Fax: (773) 373-3571

National Action Network
http://www.nationalactionnetworklv.org
3925 MLK – Suite 213
North Las Vegas, NV 89032
Telephone: (702) 646-9720 or (702) 646-9983
Fax: (702) 646-9842

GLBT RESOURCES

Human Rights Campaign
http://www.hrc.org
1640 Rhode Island Avenue, N.W.
Washington, DC 20036
Telephone: (202) 628-4160
Fax: (202) 347-5323

National Gay and Lesbian Task Force
http://www.thetaskforce.org
1325 Massachusetts Avenue, N.W.
Suite 600
Washington, DC 20005
Telephone: (202) 393-5177
Fax: (202) 393-2241

Lambda Legal Defense and Education Fund
http://www.lambdalegal.org
120 Wall Street – Suite 1500
New York, NY 10005-3905
Telephone: (212) 809-8585

Gay & Lesbian Alliance Against Defamation
http://www.glaad.org
5455 Wilshire Boulevard
Suite 1500
Los Angeles, CA 90036
Telephone: (323) 933-2240
Fax: (323) 933-2241

Parents, Families & Friends of Lesbians & Gays
http://www.pflag.org
1726 M Street, N.W.
Suite 400
Washington, DC 20036
Telephone: (202) 467-8180
Fax: (202) 467-8194

Gay Men's Health Crisis
http://www.gmhc.org
The Tisch Building
119 W. 24th Street
New York, NY 10011
Telephone: (212) 367-1000

International Gay and Lesbian Human Rights Commission
http://www.iglhrc.org
350 Fifth Avenue
34th Floor
New York, NY 10118
Telephone: (212) 216-1814
Fax: (212) 216-1876

National Center for Lesbian Rights
http://www.nclrights.org
870 Market Street
Suite 370
San Francisco, CA 94102
Telephone: (415) 392-6257
Fax: (415) 392-8442

National Black Justice Coalition
http://www.nbjcoalition.org
1725 I Street, N.W.
Suite 300
Washington, DC 20006
Telephone: (202) 349-3756

OUT Professionals
http://www.outprofessionals.org
107 W. 25th Street, 6D
New York, NY 10001
Telephone: (212) 462-9255

Latino Commission on AIDS
http://www.latinoaids.org
24 W. 25th Street
9th Floor
New York, NY 10010
Telephone: (212) 675-3288
Fax: (212) 675-3466

Gay Asian Pacific Alliance
http://www.gapa.org
P.O. Box 421884
San Francisco, CA 94142-1884
Telephone: (415) 282-4272

Al-Fatiha Foundation
http://www.al-fatiha.org
P.O. Box 33015
Washington, DC 20033
Telephone: (202) 452-5534

Queers on Wheels
http://www.queersonwheels.com/
1235 Charles Street
Pasadena, CA 91103
Telephone: (626) 578-0140
Fax: (267) 316-5797

Freedom to Marry

http://www.freedomtomarry.org
116 W. 23rd Street – Suite 500
New York, NY 10011
Telephone: (212) 851-8418
Fax: (646) 375-2069

Metropolitan Community Churches

http://www.mcchurch.org
8704 Santa Monica Boulevard
2nd Floor
West Hollywood, CA 90069
Telephone: (310) 360-8640
Fax: (310) 360-8680

RESOURCES FOR PEOPLE WITH DISABILITIES

National Organization on Disability

http://www.nod.org
910 Sixteenth Street, N.W.
Suite 600
Washington, DC 20006
Telephone: (202) 293-5960
TTY: (202) 293-5968
Fax: (202) 293-7999

Mobility International USA

http://www.miusa.org
P.O. Box 10767
Eugene, OR 97440
Telephone: (541) 343-1284 (Tel/TTY)
Fax: (541) 343-6812

Disabled Peoples' International

http://www.dpi.org
748 Broadway
Winnipeg, Manitoba, Canada
R3G OX3
Telephone: (204) 287-8010
Fax: (204) 783-6270

Disability Rights Education and Defense Fund

http://www.dredf.org
2212 Sixth Street
Berkeley, CA 94710
Telephone: (510) 644-2555 (Tel/TTY)
Fax: (510) 841-8645

Consortium for Citizens with Disabilities

http://www.c-c-d.org
1660 L Street, N.W.
Suite 700
Washington, DC 20036
Telephone: (202) 783-2229
Fax: (202) 783-8250

American Association of People with Disabilities

http://www.aapd-dc.org
1629 K Street, N.W.
Suite 503
Washington, DC 20006
Telephone: (800) 840-8844
TTY: (202) 457-0046

The Center for an Accessible Society

http://www.accessiblesociety.org
2980 Beech Street
San Diego, CA 92102
Telephone: (619) 232-2727

LATINO RESOURCES

Hispanic Alliance for Career Enhancement

http://www.hace-usa.org
25 E. Washington St. – Suite 1500
Chicago, IL 60602
Telephone: (312) 435-0498
Fax: (312) 435-1494

Hispanic Association of Corporate Responsibility

http://www.hacr.org
1444 I Street, N.W.
Suite 850
Washington, DC 20005
Telephone: (202) 835-9672
Fax: (202) 457-0455

Mexican American Legal Defense and Education Fund

http://www.maldef.org
1717 K Street, N.W.
Suite 311
Washington, DC 20036
Telephone: (202) 293-2828
Fax: (202) 293-2849

National Council of La Raza

http://www.nclr.org
1126 16th Street, N.W.
Washington, DC 20036
Telephone: (202) 785-1670

League of United Latin American Citizens (LULAC)

http://www.lulac.org
2000 L Street, N.W.
Suite 610
Washington, D.C. 20036
Telephone: (202) 833-6130
Fax: (202) 833-6135

Puerto Rican Legal Defense & Education Fund

http://www.prldef.org
99 Hudson Street
14th Floor
New York, NY 10013-2815
Telephone: (212) 219-3360
(800) 328-2322
Fax: (212) 431-4276

Institute for Puerto Rican Policy Inc.
http://www.prldef.org
99 Hudson Street
14th Floor
New York, NY 10013
Telephone: (212) 739-7516
Fax: (212) 431-4276

NATIVE AMERICAN RESOURCES

Native American Business Alliance
http://www.native-american-bus.org/
Michigan Office
30700 Telegraph Road – Suite 1675
Bingham Farms, MI 48025
Phone: (248) 988-9344
Fax: (248) 988-9348

National Congress of American Indians
http://www.ncai.org
1301 Connecticut Avenue, N.W.
Suite 200
Washington, DC 20036
Telephone: (202) 466-7767
Fax: (202) 466-7797

WOMEN'S RESOURCES

Catalyst
http://www.catalystwomen.org
New York Office
120 Wall Street
5th Floor
New York, NY 10005
Telephone: (212) 514-7600
Fax: (212) 514-8470

San Jose Office
2825 North First Street – Suite 200
San Jose, CA 95134
Telephone: (408) 435-1300
Fax: (408) 577-0425

Toronto Office
8 King Street East – Suite 505
Toronto, Ontario M5C-1B5
Telephone: (416) 815-7600
Fax: (416) 815-7601

National Association of Women Business Owners (NAWBO)
http://www.nawbo.org
8405 Greensboro Drive – Suite 800
McLean, VA 22102
Telephone: 800-55-NAWBO
(800) 226-2926

National Organization for Women
http://www.now.org
1100 H Street, N.W. – 3rd Floor
Washington, DC 20005
Telephone: (202) 628-8NOW (8669)
Fax Number: (202) 785-8576

National Council of Women's Organizations
http://www.womensorganizations.org
1050 17th Street, N.W. – Suite 250
Washington, DC 20036
Telephone: (202) 293-4505
Fax: (202) 293-4507

Business & Professional Women/USA
http://www.bpwusa.org
1900 M Street, N.W. – Suite 310
Washington, DC 20036
Telephone: (202) 293-1100
Fax: (202) 861-0298

Center For Advancement Of Public Policy
http://www.capponline.org/
1735 S. Street, N.W.
Washington, DC 20009
Phone: (202) 797-0606

Center for Health and Gender Equity
http://www.genderhealth.org/
6930 Carroll Avenue – Suite 910
Takoma Park, MD 20912
Telephone: (301) 270-1182
Fax: (301) 270-2052

Center for Women Policy Studies
http://www.centerwomenpolicy.org
1211 Connecticut Avenue, N.W. – Suite 312
Washington, DC 20036
Telephone: (202) 872-1770
Fax: (202) 296-8962

Cornell University Institute For Women & Work
http://www.ilr.cornell.edu/extension/iww/default.html
16 E. 34th Street
New York, NY 10016-4328
Telephone: (212) 340-2800
Fax: (212) 340-2822

Economist's Policy Group on Women's Issues
http://www.womensorganizations.org/indexMembers.cfm
5430 41st Place, N.W.
Washington, DC 20015
Telephone: (202) 293-4505
Fax: (202) 293-4507

Financial Women International
http://www.fwi.org
1027 W. Roselawn Avenue
Roseville, MN 55113
Telephone: (651) 487-7632
Fax: (651) 489-1322

Girls Incorporated
http://www.girlsinc.org
120 Wall Street
New York, NY 10005-3902
Telephone: (800) 374-4475

Institute for Women's Policy Research
http://www.iwpr.org
1707 L Street, N.W.
Suite 750
Washington, DC 20036
Telephone: (202) 785-5100
Fax: (202) 833-4362

MANA, A National Latina Organization
http://www.hermana.org
1725 K Street, N.W.
Suite 201
Washington, DC 20006
Telephone: (202) 833-0060
Fax: (202) 496-0588

National Association for Female Executives
http://www.nafe.com
60 E. 42nd Street
Suite 2700
New York, NY 10165
Telephone: (212) 351-6451
Fax: (212) 351-6486

National Association of Women Business Owners
http://www.nawbo.org
8405 Greensboro Drive
Suite 800
McLean, VA 22102
Telephone: (800) 55-NAWBO

National Council for Research on Women
http://www.ncrw.org
11 Hanover Square

New York, NY 10005
Telephone: (212) 785-7335
Fax: (212) 785-7350

National Hispanic Leadership Institute
http://www.nhli.org/
1901 N. Moore Street
Suite 206
Arlington, VA 22209
Telephone: (703) 527-6007
Fax: (703) 527-6009

National Women's Law Center
http://www.nwlc.org
11 Dupont Circle, N.W.
Suite 800
Washington, DC 20036-1207
Telephone: (202) 588-5180
Fax: (202) 588-5185

Women's Committee of 100
http://www.wc100.org
230 Justice Court, N.E.
Washington, DC 20002
Telephone: (202) 546-9764
Fax: (202) 363-4356

Women's Research & Education Institute
http://www.wrei.org
1750 New York Avenue, N.W.
Suite 350
Washington, DC 20006
Telephone: (202) 628-0444
Fax: (202) 628-0458

Index

NOTES